Healing pain

Feelings of loss, resulting in grief, are triggered by many situations besides the death of a loved one – for example, divorce, loss of health through accident or serious illness such as cancer or AIDS, or the birth of a handicapped child. *Healing Pain* investigates why the process of grief can be such a dramatic turning-point for those who undergo it, and why they can never remain as they were before. A bestseller in Scandinavia, it is based on ten years of intensive work with people affected by, or at risk from, both normal and pathological grief.

Nini Leick and Marianne Davidsen-Nielsen describe the original methods of treatment they have developed to help people suffering complex losses find the healing power inherent in healthy grief. Starting with a comprehensive account of the grief process and an outline of the classical models, they give detailed and practical advice on how to work with normal and pathological grief in individual or group settings. The treatment methods described can be used and adapted by all professionals who work with grief, helping them to identify people threatened by pathological grief and suggesting how to find out precisely where in the grief process the mourner may be stuck.

A moving book, clearly and simply written, *Healing Pain* is addressed to everybody who wishes to understand the feelings of grief at a deeper level. It will be of great value not only to professionals such as nurses, counsellors and social workers, but also to those encountering grief in themselves or others.

Healing pain
Attachment, loss and grief therapy

Nini Leick
and
Marianne Davidsen-Nielsen

Translated from Danish by
David Stoner

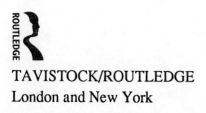
TAVISTOCK/ROUTLEDGE
London and New York

First published in Denmark in 1987

First published in Great Britain in 1991
by Routledge
11 New Fetter Lane, London EC4P 4EE

Simultaneously published in the USA and Canada
by Routledge
a division of Routledge, Chapman and Hall Inc.
29 West 35th Street, New York, NY 10001

Reprinted 1992

Typeset by LaserScript Limited, Mitcham, Surrey
Printed in Great Britain by
Biddles Ltd, Guildford and King's Lynn

British Library Cataloguing in Publication Data

Leick, Nini, 1940-
Healing Pain : attachment, loss and grief therapy.
  1. Man. Grief. Psychotherapy.
  I. Title II. Davidsen-Nielsen, Marianne, 1940- III. Den
nødvendige smerte. English
  616.8521

Library of Congress Cataloging in Publication Data

Leick, Nini, 1940-
  [Nødvendige smerte. English]
  Healing pain: attachment, loss, and grief therapy/by Nini Leick
  and Marianne Davidsen-Nielsen; translated from the Danish by David
  Stoner.
  p.   cm.
  Translation of: Den nødvendige smerte.
  Includes bibliographical references and index.
  1. Grief – Psychological aspects. 2. Bereavement – Psychological
  aspects. 3. Psychotherapy. I. Davidsen-Nielsen, Marianne, 1940–
  II. Title.
  RC455.4.L67L4513   1991   90-8509
  155.9'37–dc20   CIP

ISBN 0–415–06087–7
        0–415–04795–1 (pbk)

Ronald W. Ramsay, In Memoriam

Contents

Introduction

Why do some people emerge from grief strengthened? Why do others become strained, depressed, anxiety-ridden, or develop psychosomatic symptoms? Why is someone who is affected by grief never the same again? What kind of forces make the grief a turning-point so dramatic that our life becomes either a freer or a more restricted one?

These questions have exercised us in the ten years we have been working with people in grief and crisis. We have been able to help many on their way, and time after time they have found healing forces in their grief that have surprised both them and us. For others, the grief became the beginning of a life as patients and clients of the social and health sectors. This book deals with these questions.

In our grief and crisis project, we have had people referred to us who needed help in connection with overwhelming acute crises and periods of grief; others needed help to release the emotions of grief after losses in the recent or more remote past. Personal development has been most obvious when the clients succeeded in unravelling their symptoms from an avoided grief reaction, but even people who came to us with more recent losses – a spouse who had deserted them, a mother who was dead, a child who had been killed on the road – have been able, through the grief, to throw off old neurosis-like behaviour patterns, thus achieving greater freedom and more strength for living.

In the last nineteen years both of us have been engaged in psychotherapy individually as well as in groups. So we had a good deal of knowledge and experience of people in need and of the therapeutic processes which can relieve mental symptoms, before we began to concentrate our efforts upon grief.

However, while working on losses, traumas and the emotions of grief, we have discovered therapeutic possibilities that we had overlooked before through not focusing sufficiently on the turning-point that grief work is. These possibilities, too, are dealt with in this book.

We are both very much practitioners. The main aim of our work has

1

been to help our clients in the best way possible rather than to contribute to the formation of theories and new forms of treatment. 'Learning by doing' is what the educationist John Dewey called the method based on practical experience. The method is adjusted according to good and bad results.

In this way it is the clients who have been our true teachers in this work. It is they who have shown us the many facets of the emotions of grief. It is they who have taught us the uniformity and variety of individual grief work, and it is they who, through their development, have inspired us to find the literature which, on a deeper and more theoretical level, has helped us to understand what we were seeing.

The story behind our grief-crisis project sheds light on why we came to concern ourselves with group therapy focusing on crisis help and grief therapy. In different ways we had both been working with traumatic events. One of us especially had been interested in the traumas which affect cancer patients, and the other had worked on incest, which may also be regarded as a trauma.

During a study period in England, one of us made contact with Professor Ron Ramsay, who had specialized in the treatment of avoided grief. Later we both received inspiring teaching from him here in Denmark. These meetings with Ramsay were crucial for our later project, and they became for us an introduction to the concept of grief therapy. Ron Ramsay has since died. We dedicate this book to him with gratitude.

Our experience of group therapy with cancer patients and incest victims had shown us how mind-broadening it is for people with the same problems to share their thoughts and feelings. So is was a matter of course for us to gather people with various losses and traumas into a group focusing on their grief and crisis reactions.

In 1980 we got the chance to try out this idea of gathering clients who had problems with grief work into a therapeutic group. This was in the Student Counselling Service in Copenhagen, where we had been working in collaboration since 1972. Over four years we developed the treatment form: 'the open grief-group', which is characterized by individual treatment in a group. Later, we tested out the method for five years on a clientele who had a greater spread of both age and education than the students with whom we had been involved in the Student Counselling Service. So our experience of ten years' work with around 950 people with grief and crisis reactions forms the basis of this book.

The book has seven chapters. The subject of Chapter One is that before every loss there is an attachment. So we go back to the earliest stages of the child's development to understand what attachment is, and what emotions are triggered off by a separation. One theme is understanding how the healing grief work and weeping are bound up together.

In this theoretical chapter we also look at why some people find the reactions of grief beyond them, and why others develop through grief and crisis. We attempt to reach explanations on a psychological level different from those with which the literature of crisis and grief is usually concerned.

Chapter Two shows that grief work may be seen as four tasks which the mourner has to complete in order to be able to conclude his grief and reinvest his emotional energy in new relationships. We found this model in the work of the American psychologist J. William Worden, who in 1983 published a book on the counselling of mourners and on grief therapy. The use of the term 'tasks' underlines that grief work is a process which demands something active of the grieving person. The tasks are as follows:

The loss has to be recognized.
The various emotions of grief have to be released.
New skills have to be developed.
The emotional energy has to be reinvested.

We have found this model more usable than the phase description which is customarily employed in crisis theories and for grief work. The tasks are not phases, but intertwine with one another from start to finish of any normal grief work.

However, Worden's model is also very relevant when, with a view to intervention, we have to identify the point in his grief work at which the mourner has come to a halt. This chapter gives precise examples of how therapists can work with the various tasks.

Chapter Three discusses what group of grieving people are at risk of a pathological development of grief. We have chosen three indicators as aids in discovering who may be presumed to be at risk when affected by grief and crisis. The indicators are:

The *circumstances* around the loss.
The mourner's *personality* and *attachment* to the person or thing he has lost.
The mourner's *psycho-social* situation.

This chapter contains many concrete examples of those who belong to the risk group. At the same time there is help to be found for therapists who need to identify who needs grief help and who should be considered for grief therapy.

Chapter Four shows how the open grief group is used as a form of treatment in acute, delayed, avoided and chronic grief. We describe the advantages to be found in working in a group, how the group may function as a temporary network, and the role of the therapists in the group.

Chapter Five deals with crisis intervention and grief therapy. Examples are given of how a therapist may carry out crisis intervention in connection with a traumatic event. A number of concrete examples of grief therapy in relation to *delayed* and *avoided* grief are examined. Therapeutic work with chronic grief and special problems related to alcohol abuse and grief are also touched upon.

This chapter may be used as a catalogue for therapists in need of ideas on possible ways of tackling losses and traumas. Personal and professional qualifications for working with people in grief are also touched upon.

Chapter Six is about a woman and the individual grief therapy which she underwent about a year after her husband committed suicide. She gives her own description of the course of the therapy and of how her children reacted.

Chapter Seven deals with other kinds of losses than deaths. Divorce, handicaps, having a handicapped child and life-threatening illness are examples of ambiguous losses when the grief work is often neglected because the loss is not recognized. The four tasks of grief work must be completed whatever loss has to be undergone, and so in principle there is no difference between various kinds of loss. But we have chosen to survey various grief therapies in relation to what we call 'unclear' losses, because many therapists feel uncertain in these areas. We have selected losses in connection with the disease of muscular atrophy and blindness, delayed grief in connection with having a handicapped child, and cancer as an example of potentially terminal disease. The concept of 'ongoing grief' is presented here, and the theme of hope, grief work and life-threatening disease is also treated. Finally, a young gay man describes the loss he felt on being diagnosed as HIV positive. He too had to complete grief work to get the strength to go on living.

We have indicated that we have a number of different aims in writing this book. It is also our intention to *heighten awareness* that people's mental problems can be caused by unresolved grief. So we have chosen to designate as pathological those grief reactions that are not natural, well knowing that the boundaries between what is normal and abnormal are fluid. But it is our impression that many therapists overlook indications that the natural grief process is not functioning. So there is too little intervention, and for this reason we have chosen a terminology which focuses on the abnormal.

All too frequently the grieving person develops symptoms that are treated with tranquillizers and anti-depressants, but this is rarely the kind of treatment that is required. There is a need for crisis help, grief help, crisis intervention and grief therapy in order to mobilize the mourner's healthy forces when the grief process is being blocked or is so difficult that the process is turning pathological.

In the following we will define what we mean by these key concepts, so that they are quite clear before we commence the seven chapters outlined above. *Crisis help* is the giving of 'first aid' when the loss or the traumatic experience is so overwhelming that the emotions 'submerge' the crisis victim; to dare to stand beside the mourner, so that he does not feel alone in his chaotic situation. Crisis help is both physical and mental care. It is a hot drink, a blanket, an affectionate arm. Crisis help is a task for both the private network and for the physician, minister, social worker or other professional helper who may be involved.

Crisis intervention is the term for active professional measures that may be necessary in the first period after a loss. Crisis intervention may involve confronting the mourner with his loss so that his emotions are released. It may be interposing firmly and directively in the total life-setting of the bereaved, because the crisis state entails that the person's ordinary problem-solving ability has been put out of action. It requires that the helper dares to be vigorous, dominant and directive, and dares to use his professional identity as a justification for his actions. Crisis intervention is thus a breach of style compared with other forms of psycho-social and therapeutic treatment.

Grief help is longer-term support in the four tasks of grief work. Grief work is a demanding, tough process. From time to time the mourner will be very uncertain and vulnerable. Here, both the network and the therapist may make an important preventive contribution by realizing where the mourner is faltering and giving him help in making progress. The support of being in a grief group is an example of grief help.

Grief therapy is the form of treatment which can help grievers who cannot themselves cope with the separation from the person or thing they have lost, and so are not getting the four tasks completed. Grief therapy is work on delayed, avoided or chronic grief. Grief therapy is short-term therapy that can be carried out by therapists who are both able to be emotionally confrontational and who have psychotherapeutic experience.

We have omitted the concept of crisis therapy, because it is confusing and imprecise. If the mourner is in a crisis, there is need for *crisis help* or *crisis intervention*. It is a reliable rule of thumb that there is *always* grief in crisis, but there is not necessarily crisis in grief. In practice this means that the help that may be called for after the crisis help or crisis intervention may be grief help or grief therapy, depending on how one assesses the risk of a pathological grief development. Thus the concept of crisis therapy becomes superfluous.

Most literature on grief and mourning quotes Cullberg's model, which divides the crisis into four phases which follow consecutively in time. They are called the shock phase, the reaction phase, the repair phase and the new-orientation phase. Our experience is that in the beginning it can be confusing to anyone accustomed to using a phase model like this as a frame of reference to replace it with the four tasks of grief work.

So we want to reiterate that the tasks intertwine from the moment the loss has taken place. The recognition of the loss and the feelings that follow can, especially at the beginning, develop into a crisis state in which crisis help or crisis intervention may be necessary as part of the help in completing the four tasks.

So this is a book about the treatment of losses and traumas. In Greek a 'trauma' is a wound, a lesion. Here it means a lesion of the mind, an upheaval in the soul. Thus a traumatic train of events is one with perturbing experiences. The kind of losses we deal with here are all traumatic. They are traumas which become turning-points in people's lives – turning-points that may become growth points if the emotions of the grief are released.

We have found an old Jewish story which poetically contains the message that is ours in this book.

The first tear

When Adam and Eve were driven out of the Garden of Eden, God saw that they repented of their transgression. He felt pity for them, and gently said: 'Poor children! I have punished you for your offences and have driven you out of the Garden of Eden, where you lived without grief and worry. Now you are entering a world full of grief and unhappiness that defies description. But you shall know that I am generous and that my love for you will last for ever. I know that you will encounter much adversity and it will embitter your lives. Therefore I bestow upon you my most precious treasure, this costly pearl – the tear. When you are overwhelmed by grief, when your hearts are about to break and great pain is clutching your soul, then this tear will fall from your eyes, and the burden will at once be easier to bear.'

At these words Adam and Eve became numb with grief. Tears welled forth from their eyes, streamed down their cheeks, and fell upon the ground.

And it was these tears of pain which first moistened the earth. Adam and Eve left behind a precious inheritance to their children. And ever since, when someone is in great grief, his heart is in pain and his mind is heavy, tears flow from his eyes. And behold! the grief eases.

Chapter one

On attachment, loss and grief

'You have to walk on the earth even if it is glowing,' an old woman once said. The earth beneath us feels on fire when we are stricken by serious losses and traumas. We are overwhelmed by pain, tears, guilt feelings, anger and fear. Difficulty in sleeping, palpitations, indigestion, body aches – all are symptoms that the autonomous nervous system has been disturbed.

What kind of forces are released by grief and crisis? Forces which may be so violent that soul and body are threatened? This question became more and more insistent as we worked with the grief group. We sought for a frame of reference which could explain the pathological development of grief with its physical and mental symptoms as well as healthy grief work with its potential for personal growth.

We know that when people grieve it is because they have lost someone or something to which they were closely attached. This means that, before any loss, there have been affinity and attachment. So we looked for inspiration in those researchers who have particularly concerned themselves with attachment between humans and with losses and traumas. We found elements for constructing a whole in John Bowlby, Erik H. Erikson, Sigmund Freud, Alexander Lowen, Eric Lindemann, Irvin D. Yalom, Alice Miller and in the researcher who wrote an epoch-making work on the symptoms of those who have suffered grief, Colin Murray Parkes.

Affinity and attachment processes

People can be attached to a multiplicity of things: human beings, money, job, prestige, home, land and other possessions. Appearance and health are often taken for granted, but if someone loses a breast or an arm or becomes seriously ill, then they understand the great importance of their attachment to the body and its condition.

In what does this attachment process consist? The attachment between people is the most important to understand, as it is usually the loss of someone close to us that triggers off the deepest grief. The English psychiatrist John Bowlby has researched into attachment and separation throughout his life. He has gathered all his reflections and experience into the three-volume work *Attachment and Loss*.

Bowlby regards a close attachment to one or more people as just as important as food and drink. A baby is born with the ability to develop behaviour patterns that make his mother respond. For instance, a baby quickly learns that as a rule his crying will bring his mother to him. Later he begins to smile and thus obtains another form of attention. Gradually he can hold tightly, follow her, seek and call. The goal of this contacting behaviour is to have his mother in the close proximity which gives the child most security. This may be contact as close as sitting on her lap if he is afraid or upset. If he is three years old, it may be enough for her to be within sight. Later the optimum distance may be within earshot. Age and needs are continually changing the distance which gives the 'appropriate' security. Adolescence is a period in which the youngster is uncertain of the optimum distance, but attachment to parents is still crucial to his development. Later new bonds are normally developed to a partner, children and friends. Bowlby stresses that individual needs for a close attachment with a flexible optimum distance vary throughout life.

In his description of the young child's development, Erik Erikson has laid stress on some of the same factors as Bowlby, but uses somewhat different words. He sees a person's lifelong development as a long series of development crises. In each of these crises there is an emotional dilemma to be solved. We shall here look at Erikson's first two stages of development, which correspond to Bowlby's attachment period, namely, the child's development up to 3 years. Erikson sees the child's first dilemma as how to achieve a *feeling of basic trust* and overcome the feeling of basic distrust. This gives a basis for *hope*. Basic trust arises through affinity with those closest, often the mother. This attachment is created if the child can securely expect that his mother will return when she goes away, will be there when she is needed, and that if the child cries, calls or looks for her, he will be able to get hold of her.

The child's next developmental dilemma is achieving a *feeling of independence* – and combating a feeling of doubt and shame. In this way *will* is engendered. From the age of 18 months to about 3 years, the child begins to discover that he is in control of his own behaviour and develops a feeling of independence. The conflict lies in the extent to which the child can deploy his independence while yet maintaining his dependence upon his parents. At this stage of development, living means trying to do everything on one's own: eating, dressing, opening and closing things and so on. The parents' openness to allowing the child liberty in some areas and their ability to lay down firm norms in others will be reflected in the child's tolerance and self-confidence. If the child is over-inhibited or given too wide a scope, he may develop a gradually growing feeling of shame and doubt about himself and his abilities. The experience which the child has had in these two phases determines how in the future he will be able to attach himself to other people and how flexible he will be in the matter of finding the 'optimum distance'. People work all their lives on this problem. If people have not emerged fairly successfully from these two stages of development, they will become rigid in their efforts to find the 'optimum distance'. Their relationships will either become too close (symbiotic), too distant or ambivalent.

Bereavements injure our feeling of affinity and attachment to others and so affect us vitally. It is therefore very understandable that people who have previously had difficulties in their attachment process also have problems in living through the emotions of grief in a healing way. Because their *basic trust* has been undermined, it is hard for them to dare to say goodbye to one of their dear ones and to welcome new contacts. Their difficulty in finding the optimum distance also means that they have problems in making effective use of a network, and this may have consequences for the way their grief work proceeds. So the work of both Bowlby and Erikson gives a good and sound explanation of why it is so stressful for us human beings to lose our attachment.

Bereavements and grief work

In 1917 Freud wrote an article on grief called 'Trauer und Melancholi'. This became crucial because he introduced two important concepts for understanding the nature of grief. He used the term 'object loss' to describe losing something or someone to whom one is attached. The goal of the grief is to break the bond which exists between the griever (the subject) and the deceased (the object). This demands a heavy psychological input from the mourner, and so Freud calls this process *grief work*.

Another classic contribution to the understanding of grief came from the American psychiatrist Eric Lindemann. In 1944 he studied the reactions of the bereaved after a serious fire disaster in which about 500 people perished. He was the first to describe the physical and mental symptomatology of acute grief, and demonstrated that people's reaction patterns when the grief is released are remarkably uniform. His work thus became a foundation for our being able to distinguish between normal and pathological grief reactions.

The normal course of grief consists on a superior level of three phases: deliverance from *the past* by recognizing the significance of the loss in all its facets; re-building of *the present* with a new everyday life that contains both what is left and some necessary changes; and an experience of having a *future* with new possibilities, new pathways. It is a long, tough and painful process, which may be so turbulent that in a frightening way we may feel that we are 'out of our wits'. It is called a state of crisis when someone is so much 'out of their wits' because of the traumatic event that for a while they cannot use their ordinary problem-solving ability. They are emotionally overwhelmed, confused and needing the help of others to be able to cope. In other words, for some period of time they are dependent upon a network.

In 1972 Colin M. Parkes published the book *Bereavement: Studies of Grief in Adult Life* that was epoch-making for research into grief reactions. In it he gathered his experience from an investigation into widows' grief reactions and gave a detailed description of the many constituent processes of which the normal grief work consists. What has particularly interested us about Parkes's writings is his close collaboration with Bowlby, who inspired him to take as his starting-point for a better understanding of the grief process the attachment there was between the mourner and the deceased.

As mentioned, Bowlby stresses that part of the child's behaviour is aimed at creating and retaining contact with the mother. It cries, seeks, calls, smiles, grips, holds on, and so on. Bowlby and Parkes agree that part of the mourner's behaviour may be understood as an attempt to make contact with or in some more unconscious way to hold on to the deceased. Weeping may thus be a way of summoning the deceased, just as the baby cries to summon his mother.

Weeping

In our work on loss and traumas the great importance of weeping in grief work has become more and more evident. We have also increasingly realized that the weeping may have various purposes. The calling weeping which Bowlby describes is attempting to hold on to the person or thing which has been lost. It is a shallower weeping, because the breathing is rapid, and it does not bring the same relief as does the deep weeping which occurs when someone begins to let go of the deceased. Thus human beings have both a 'calling weeping' and a 'letting-go weeping'.

Weeping is important, because in the tears there are forces that heal both physically and mentally. In the old Jewish story told in the Introduction, the tear is designated the most precious treasure, a costly pearl, because 'when someone is in great grief, his heart is in pain, and his mind is heavy, tears flow from his eyes. And behold! the grief eases'.

In all its simplicity this story emphasizes that tears have a relieving effect on the stress produced by loss and trauma. The founder of bioenergetics, Alexander Lowen, describes it like this:

Weeping accompanied by sobbing is the first and deepest release of tensions. Children can weep almost from the moment of birth and weep without trouble in connection with all stress influences that produce a state of tension in the body. First the child's body is tensed, then its jaw trembles, and immediately afterwards it breaks out in a convulsion-like release of tension. Man is the only animal that can react to stress and tensions in this way.

However, this innate ability to reduce stress through weeping is increasingly obstructed as most people grow up. John Bowlby, Erik H. Erikson and Alexander Lowen all stress how harmful it is when adults disapprove of children's tears by saying, for instance, 'It's nothing to cry about'. In this way they impair the children's ability to grieve and thus to resolve the stresses in a wholesome and natural way. Some children gradually learn to control themselves so well that as adults they never weep. Others can be tearful but without ever daring to give way to releasing weeping. These people often feel that they weep too much, but they never achieve any true relief. It may be presumed that their weeping resembles the 'calling for mother' which we mentioned before, and it does not give the same release of tension as the deep weeping. We have often seen just this continual, rather shallow weeping in people in chronic grief – that is, those who will not let go of the thing or person they have lost. Alexander Lowen writes about this:

If weeping becomes continuous, it means that there is a constant tension in the body. And as a result of this tension there is also a lasting state of grief.... It is not the frequency of the grief, but its depth, that determines the release that it may bring.

Weeping that heals is thus the profound sobbing in which, like a baby, someone lets go of tensions in the body. The tensions arise from the muscles of the body contracting as a defence against both physical and mental pain. This contraction occurs so that, at the moment the trauma occurs, the pain does not become too overwhelming for the body's usual balance in the autonomic nervous system. We have to preserve our ability to act in the face of a threat while it is going on. The pain arises when the tension in the muscles starts to be released. This normally happens when the very acute situation is past. A parallel is the state of mental shock which protects the person against being over-whelmed by the situation. The realization penetrates more slowly, and this is of course useful.

However, the healthy state of balance in the body depends on the tensions being released again. This occurs when we give way to the pain

11

and start to weep. We may compare this process with orgasm, which is also a dissolution of a state of tension in the body. The function of weeping is thus to dissolve the bodily tensions which the loss or trauma has caused in the musculature of the body.

Weeping has various depths and thus various qualities of release of muscle tension. People who find it hard to weep have to go through a process in which the weeping gradually becomes deeper and deeper the more they dare to give way to it. Tears always have some tension-releasing value for the moment, but it is only the more profound weeping that gives a longer-lasting feeling of relief.

Deep relieving weeping does not come until one is willing finally to let go of what one has lost. In bioenergetics it is thought that it may also unleash chronic tensions which derive from old unprocessed traumas. Tears probably have another function too, for they help to restore the body's natural balance in connection with stress. Investigations show that the chemical content of the tears in weeping is different from that of tears from eyes that are 'watering'. It is not yet known how they fit physiologically into the body's restoration in connection with the grief process.

Despite the fact that weeping is an important part of our healthy mental equipment, we know that many people find it difficult to weep. This applies to shallow weeping and more particularly to profound sobbing. There are a number of explanations why not everyone is able to utilize their innate resources in order to heal the wounds in the psyche which losses and traumas cause.

Wounds in the psyche

There is an obvious comparison between psychical wounds and bodily wounds. We say of the bereaved, 'It was a hard blow for her' or 'He was knocked out by it'. People around treat mourners rather as they do the physically ill. They get sick leave for days or weeks, other people make the daily decisions for them, and people speak in lowered voices when they are near them.

The English psychiatrist George Engel was the first person to compare loss with a physical wound. In both cases the wound has to heal up, and that takes time. In the case of major wounds, a scar has to form. Engel sees grief work as the healthy process which slowly heals the wound in the psyche. A physical wound may fester if the regenerating forces do not act as they should. In the same way the healing forces of grief may be out of action.

In 1961 Engel wrote a controversial article in a journal of psycho-somatic medicine. He called it 'Is Grief a Disease?'. No, grief is not a disease, but it can develop into one. It is possible to die of a 'broken heart'.

Parkes's first famous investigation showed that mortality increased 40 per cent in widowers over the age of 54 in the first six months after the death. Many later investigations show similarly that people in grief and crisis are both physically and mentally under greater threat than others. In other words, it is vital to use the healing forces in the grief work in the best possible way, otherwise the wound may 'fester' – the grief process can become pathological with a risk of mental and/or physical illness.

In the USA in recent years a good deal of research has been done into the link between loss, stress and cancer. Many people consider they can demonstrate a connection between the onset of cancer and the loss of close kin. Carl Simonton, the cancer researcher, is working on the psychological stress factors which affect the immune system. He sees, for instance, a link between unprocessed loss, stress and illness. In Denmark, the American psychologist John Schneider has worked on the same range of problems. Research in the area is not unambiguous, however. There is great disagreement in medical circles about the connection between stress and disease. In our work we find that individuals who have undergone pathological grief are so stress-affected that we can be in no doubt that purely somatically they must be in the danger zone.

Forces which militate against healthy grief work

Why do so many people avoid deep weeping? Is it only because they learned as children that it is not the done thing to cry? Or is it also because they are afraid of getting into a state that reminds them of the time when as infants they were helpless and dependent on other people, a time when they fought to overcome the feeling of chaos by attaching themselves to their mother? It is frightening for an adult to give way and feel once more like a small and helpless child.

If we lose someone close to us, such as a spouse or a child, there is much in the situation that is reminiscent of the baby's helplessness. One of those on whom the mourner had based the content of his life and his security has gone. The mourner is left unhappy and frightened. It is often expressed like this: 'It's like losing part of myself.' It often seems that his attachment to anybody but the one he has lost has become unimportant. 'Now I have nobody left that I am fond of,' said a mother whose youngest child had died. She still had four other children! She was like a crying child whose mother had abandoned her. A mourner who completely gives way to his weeping may resemble a little child. 'I felt like putting my arms round her, she seemed so helpless,' said a trainee in our group about a weeping woman who had lost her baby.

It takes courage to make such a profound regression. In glimpses it seems as if the mourner is returning to a much earlier stage of his development. The despair and the sense of chaos may be so profound that it seems as if his basic trust in other people has to be built up again from scratch. So it is quite crucial for the mourner to have people around who can accommodate the grief and support the griever in his helplessness.

During the periods when the mourner gives way to the emotions of grief, there must be people able to give hope that new forms of attachment are possible in the future.

Grief work as an opportunity for development

People who have difficulties with what Erik Erikson calls *basic trust* and Bowlby calls the *optimum distance* to others often need professional help in their grief work. They find it especially hard to let go of control. In their earliest childhood they experienced fear, emptiness and the feeling of being abandoned, and they know intuitively that they risk experiencing these feelings again if they give up control. As adults they have attached themselves to others in an unhealthy and rigid way.

In the introduction to this book we mentioned that grief work is always a turning-point in a person's life. In our work with people suffering from pathological grief, we have particularly seen the turning-point as a change in the mourner's relation to other people. The loss either brings about increased insecurity and great problems about distance to others or it is an opportunity to establish more healthy relationships with greater flexibility. *This comes about by the mourner being given opportunity in the grief therapy to meet loneliness, anxiety and emptiness in a context in which he feels understood and supported.* If we set this alongside Erik Erikson's first two stages of child development, it would seem that the process of sharing the deep pain with others may help to repair the damage from childhood. The mourner achieves first an increase of basic security. Later a greater feeling of independence develops from his being able to take leave of the deceased. The Swiss psychoanalyst Alice Miller has been another source of inspiration in our efforts to understand why people can emerge from even very serious bereavements with enhanced health and vitality.

The lost self

Wounds in the psyche and healing grief work have also been at the centre of Alice Miller's work. Three of her books – *The Drama of Being a Child, For Your Own Good* and *Thou Shalt Not Be Aware* – have greatly influenced our view of the therapeutic possibilities in grief work.

John Bowlby and Alice Miller both look upon psychoanalysis as their foundation and have both, after a lifetime's work on the concepts of psychoanalysis, found it necessary to make some revision of them in various areas. What has been most intriguing to us is that, apparently independently, they agree on the great importance for the child's development of external losses and traumas. It is not the traumatic occurrence itself that leaves its traces, but *the way the parents accommodate the child's emotional reaction to the loss or trauma.*

Again and again in her books Alice Miller emphasizes that it is crucial for a child's psychological development that he is given the opportunity to express his feelings clearly and plainly. The adults must be able to accommodate the child's many and varied emotions, not only of joy and sorrow, but also of jealousy, greed, meanness and so on. Only through the adult's acceptance and reflection of the child's register of emotions can the child learn for himself to know and thus shape his true self, his true identity. She stresses that losses and traumas in childhood need not lead to neurotic development. If a child is given the opportunity with an understanding adult to express his grief and anger, then the wound left by the loss or trauma will be healed. But 'the denied trauma is a wound that can never form a scar and which can at any time begin to bleed again. Given understanding surroundings this wound can become visible and be healed,' writes Alice Miller.

The central concept in Alice Miller's writings is the *effacement of the self*. Many parents are not capable of accommodating their children's emotions; in fact, they are provoked by them. Consciously or unconsciously the parents expect instead that the children will meet the emotional needs of the adults. If the child makes his parents feel at ease, then he is 'a good child'. If he has his own wishes that run counter to those of his parents, he risks being regarded as egoistic and inconsiderate. Under these circumstances, if the child wishes to hold on to his parents' love (and what child can afford to lose that?), he very quickly learns to be a giver to his parents, making sacrifices and denying himself, long before genuine sharing and true renunciation are at all possible. 'A child who has been allowed to be egoistic, acquisitive, and antisocial long enough, later acquires a spontaneous joy in sharing and giving,' writes Alice Miller in *The Drama of Being a Child*. The parents have a need for the 'good child' who loves and admires them. The child must play this role in order to retain his parents' attention. He becomes a past master at registering the adults' feelings and needs. The price is the loss of his *self*. That means that the child has to give up understanding, indeed even registering, his own emotions. If the parents had been able to accommodate the child's variety of emotions, the self might have remained alive. To hold on to one's mother is a necessity for surviving. When the mother cannot tolerate the child's emotions, the child then effaces these emotions and thus loses part of his soul.

When the child has grown up, the price has to be paid in anxiety, depression, emptiness, indifference. These are more or less the same symptoms that we see in adults with a pathological grief reaction.

We have already referred to the first two stages in Erik Erikson's developmental theory. Here are the eight points which Alice Miller propounds in *The Drama of Being a Child*. Although Erikson and Miller do not use quite the same terms, they are in good agreement.

1   It is a fundamental need in a child to be regarded, respected and taken seriously as the person he is at any given time, and as the centre of his own activity. This is a narcissistic but legitimate need, whose fulfilment is crucial for a healthy self-image (healthy narcissism).

2   The young child's emotions and 'internal sensations' form the nucleus of the self. It is the centre and point of crystallization of the self-image.

3   In an atmosphere of respect and tolerance for the child's feelings, the child can, in the separation phase, give up symbiosis with his mother and take the step to personality development and independence.

4   For these prerequisites for healthy narcissism to be present, these children's parents must themselves have been respected as children.

5   Parents who were not respected as children for the people they were, are narcissistically deprived; that is, they seek all their lives for what their parents could not give them at the right time: a person devoted to them, taking them quite seriously, admiring them and watching them.

6   This quest cannot of course be completely successful, for it is addressed to a situation in the past that cannot be recalled; that is, the first period of self formation.

7   A person who has an unsatisfied or unconscious need is under constraint to try to get the need satisfied with surrogates.

8   One's own children are best suited to this role. A neonate is left to the mercies of his parents, and as the baby's existence depends on obtaining their attention, it will do everything not to lose this. From the very first day it will exploit all its possibilities, like a tender plant that turns towards the sun to survive.

In her books Alice Miller expounds the therapeutic process which may slowly guide the client back into contact with his original genuine feelings. The central element in her method is the client's grief work over the emotionally deprived childhood which can never be done over again. The loss is irrevocable. This may be a lengthy process, because idealization of the inaccessible parents must first be slowly broken down before recognition of the painful reality of childhood can emerge.

All their lives – or until they come for treatment – these people have retained a strong hope that their parents will sometime see them as they are, and will thus understand them and value all they have done for their parents. This wish is not fulfilled, because the parents rarely change with age. If we are not shown acceptance as children, we will as adults seek it from other people – primarily from our partner and our children. We hope that they can give us the love and acceptance we were never given by our parents. If we are not given it here, we may find solace in alcohol, pills, work and so on.

The personality traits which Alice Miller describes as resulting from the repression of self correspond more or less to the personality traits which John Bowlby and Colin Murray Parkes have found in people with pathological grief. So we must reckon that Alice Miller has shown us a picture of the childhood of some of the people who are threatened with pathological grief development. They have problems with attachments to other people. The attachment may either be much too close (symbiotic), much too distant (remote, apparent indifference), or alternatively too close or too distant (ambivalent). A more nuanced account of this will be given in the chapter on risk groups.

Grief therapy as a possible way back to the self

Alice Miller's therapeutic method is the rather slow one of psycho-analysis, which may last a number of years. In her book *Thou Shalt Not Be Aware* she enquires about other, quicker methods, which she feels must exist.

It is our view that grief therapy may be such an alternative. If someone has had an emotionally deprived childhood, he has poor chances of living through the necessary and healing pain on his own. But just because the loss of a father or mother, a spouse or a child is so dramatic, it does give an opportunity for getting through to the genuine emotions relatively quickly in a different way than is possible at other times of life.

A network that is prepared, through understanding empathy, to accommodate all the mourner's conflicting emotions of pain, anger, guilt, shame, perhaps jealousy and vengefulness and so on, may give the mourner an experience which heals part of the childhood trauma. Grief over the person lost may be the start of making contact with one's genuine emotions. That the mourner does dare to feel the pain is because the network backs up what is healthy in the process.

Often this benign network does not exist. So it has to be replaced by a therapist or, perhaps even better, by a therapy group. It then becomes the therapist or group who encourage the grieving person to re-live the complex feelings connected with the loss and to approach the final farewell. Particularly when the grief is over the loss of a parent, a spouse or a child, it is our hypothesis that this grief also contains part of the grief over the emotional needs that were not met in childhood, needs which the person has ever since been hoping to have satisfied by those closest to him. An example is as follows:

Twenty-two-year-old Catrine was referred to us in a state of confusion and despair after obtaining an abortion. In the grief group she discovered that the child she had lost represented a dream of the security she had never been given by her mother. The baby was to have been the person who could love and accept her as she was. As part of her therapeutic work in the grief group she wrote a letter to her mother in her diary. The grief work which Alice Miller describes as healing for the wounds of childhood can hardly be described more clearly than here:

'Mum, I'm sitting here crying, the pain is so intense. I am so afraid of cracking up, afraid that when I say goodbye to the hope, to you, I shall not be any more. For so many years it has been the main thing in my life, what I spent all my strength and all my time on, so I'm shatteringly, sickeningly afraid of letting go of it, of you. It is my inner image: someone who hopes. The day I don't hope any more, will I be there any more? Or will I really break into a thousand bits and vanish into the black sea of pain, loneliness and hatred? Or will I be finally free, free to feel, think, believe and have opinions on my own premisses and not as now on your and Daddy's premisses. I hereby opt for believing that I shall be free. Free of snakes, spiders and murder, free of what they represent: fear, that great fundamental fear of everything and nothing in my life. Free of and free from the compulsive idea and feeling that I must not live, really live.

And now I suppose you're asking yourself, Mum, what sort of a hope this is. It is the hope of getting you and your love. It is the hope of being accepted, loved and wanted, the hope that one day you will come towards me and pick me up, caress and cuddle me, play with me, allow me to be and to be wanted.

Saying goodbye to the hope is also facing up to the fact that you have misused me, crippled me, deserted me. Facing up to it that I was not and am not wanted, wanted because I am me. I am wanted as long as I take your problems, your anxiety, your guilt on my shoulders, I found that out when I was quite young. If I took all your burden, and left the little girl in the lurch, then I was wanted, and because I wanted so intensely to be wanted, I stupidly left the little girl in the lurch. So I have become the child who was never allowed to be a child, while you are the grown-up who never wanted to be grown-up.

You thought, and still think today, that it was ideal. Yes, for you, but bloody well not for me. You were so absorbed in your own despair and your own grief, that you did not see and would not see your own children's despair. You had to find a scapegoat and a scratching-post for all the evil in your life, and they were me and my brothers and sisters.

But how about it now, Mum? I am here lonely, afraid, in despair, and with the confounded pain you have caused me. And now I'm saying goodbye to the hope and hallo to life, for thank heaven it's always true that a goodbye is followed by a hallo.

Goodbye hope, goodbye wasted years full of hope, goodbye to the fear of not being up to it, goodbye to the terror of my life, goodbye to hatred, to abuse, abuse both of myself and of drink, goodbye to loneliness, goodbye Mum.

Goodbye to the want of you, Mum.

The want that is driving me mad, the want of a place to belong, of a lap that is mine, a home that is mine. Why did you let me down like this, what have I done to you? I really did try everything, I did everything for your sake. You're like an elastic band, if I don't let go of you completely, you'll flick back into my face. Goodbye, Mum.'

Catrine's letter to her mother shows how grief can create access to the emotions that were repressed in childhood. Catrine's grief work over the baby she did not have became a decisive turning-point in her life. Despite her youth, she had already been abusing alcohol for some years. The grief opened her defence against the necessary pain which she was then capable of feeling, because she had the grief group as a network. She did not need to escape from the emotions through drink as she had been doing for most of her adult life.

Thus Catrine was given the chance of discovering a little bit of her *true self* through the grief. At the same time she was starting on the grief at having to bid farewell to her lifelong hope of getting her childhood's emotional needs satisfied. The course of Catrine's therapy is one of the many examples we have looked at in which grief work can touch the deepest levels of the personality, because it loosens some of the avoided emotions of childhood. However, Catrine's grief work over her lost childhood will come and go in the course of her lifetime, whenever she suffers another loss, great or small. She has suffered an ambiguous loss, and we call this particular kind of grief work 'ongoing' (see Chapter Seven).

Julie gives another example in her farewell letter to the group. In the group she had been working on her feelings in connection with an unwanted divorce. Julie writes:

I have drawn up the contents of this letter several times both in my thoughts and aloud to myself – actually right from a month after I had started in this group. Then I was afraid of having to stop coming to the group – I am not afraid today, even though I have had and still have in the group a place where I can allow my feelings to come out. I still find it hard to allow this when I am at home and with other people. Some of the feelings do come out anyway in the form of outbursts of anger, palpitations and edginess. But it is through you that today I can allow myself to cry without feeling that it is tantamount to letting everything collapse. My anger, too, I can stand seeing – at least a little bit of it – without feeling such a bad conscience afterwards that I feel unworthy of life. So there have been changes in my image of myself and my way of showing my feelings, but I have to remind myself of these advances every day – reading this out is just such a reminder, and that is why I have so often re-worded this letter.

I ended by facing up to my anger, but the first few times it was weeping which came out instead, and before long, besides my anger and grief that my husband did not want to live with me and our son any more, I had also seen how neglected had been my demands in childhood for security and care. I saw that, besides having been given little support by my parents, they had demanded extensive loyalty, understanding, consideration and responsibility from me. And of course I had to become the genteel, well-bred lady that my mother so much wanted to be, and the happy, talented daughter my father needed to have. I became so genteel that you would think I had grown up somewhere else than at home, and so clever that my parents felt threatened and put out. So I had to make sure that in every situation they felt on top and never felt upset on my account – and I managed that partly by parroting their words, partly by being unreasonably uncertain of myself and by being abject.

I do not know whether it is a protest or a cry for attention on my part that I go on being like that. In that way I conceal at least from other people and not least from myself how strong I really am. By realizing this I have quite slowly been able to change it, and here the work form in this group has helped me to be able to talk about myself and to take *my* feelings and thoughts seriously – to take unto myself the right to be there.

The losses of adult life – here, a traumatic divorce – may thus become a new chance to reconquer a depth in the emotional life that was devastated in early childhood.

In Julie's great grief at losing her husband she felt that she was losing part of herself. Her self-image and security were attached to the husband she had lost. Without him she felt helpless. The security and interest which Julie had not received from her parents when a child, she had looked for from her husband. At the same time as she lost him and mourned the loss, she made connection with the loss she had suffered when as a child she lost her parents' interest. As the letter shows, she was able through these two pieces of grief work slowly to get close to her true self.

Grief work as a general opportunity for growth

It is not humanly possible to give a young child total acceptance and the mirroring of the emotional life that would be the optimum. So we have all lost part of our selves, the amount depending on the capacity of those closest to us. Fortunately, most children do not only have their parents around them. A grandmother, a good nursery-school teacher, the mother of a playmate may also play their part in giving the child some opportunity for holding on to his feelings.

It is our hypothesis that the growth that is described in the literature as a result of crisis or grief is in fact bound up with the fact that all of us have suffered some loss of self in our childhood. In our adult life we have all in various ways sought to compensate for the loss by seeking attention and love from partners, children, friends, colleagues and others. Deep down, most people have an inkling that there is no hope that this yearning for unconditional love will ever be satisfied.

Grief work may support a liberation from this longing in a number of ways. If the grief is so intense that it can break through the old emotionally deprived pattern, then the person may for the first time since early childhood find himself accommodating strong, genuine emotions. A network of people who can support and cope with the strong emotions without being alarmed will then have the function which the parents should have had when the child was small. The adult then experiences what he ought to have experienced in childhood: his whole register of strong emotions being accepted by another person. In this way the emotions become less frightening and more acceptable to himself. So a process takes place which may be the first step in turning the childhood spiral of growing fear of emotions into a new spiral in which emotions are given greater and greater room. This is a more detailed way of describing why the mourner's basic trust in others is increased.

When we live through the strong emotions connected with an irrevocable farewell, then the death of a parent, a partner or someone equally important faces us with the fact that we must live our lives without having the yearning for unconditional love satisfied by the deceased. Our grief work gives us the chance to mourn that it was not possible as an adult to get what one did not get as a child.

We discover that we can manage with less than the unconditional and yet value what we have received from a caring network. In this way we can release a quantity of energy which from childhood we have had bound up in longing or in suppressing our longing. In our experience, this new energy manifests itself in an optimism and fearlessness towards life and in an ability both to be alone and to enjoy the company of others. It may perhaps be said that we have again been given the opportunity to work on the dilemma in Erikson's second phase and to increase our feeling of independence and initiative. To use Bowlby's expression, through the emotions of grief we are again working to find the 'optimum distance' to other people.

As a conclusion to this chapter we want to return to the theme of control/chaos, meaning/meaninglessness. A person's need to feel control, coherence and meaning in his life is great. From our earliest childhood we have been learning to master our life, learning to overcome chaos. Traumatic events mobilize our fear that the chaos will devour us. The emotions of grief are experienced by giving up control, giving way, abandoning ourselves to the feeling of chaos. The encounter with chaos and the uncontrollable aspect of existence paradoxically gives us strength and courage to live. A young woman who had lost both her mother and her sister revealed that in spite of her intense encounter with unhappiness and death in the grief group she was leaving it with a sense that life had become less dangerous.

The American psychiatrist Irvin D. Yalom approaches psychotherapy from an existential point of view, and his theories have made it possible for us to understand the process of mourning from one more angle.

Yalom's four concepts

Yalom has based his book *Existential Psychotherapy* on four concepts: death, freedom, isolation and meaninglessness. They represent four basic conflicts, which each person must face in the course of his life because they are givens of existence. He views neurosis and malfunction as a result of the individual's inability to come to terms with one or more of the four conflicts. We propose that one of the reasons why grief work is so demanding and so frightening is that the mourner has to confront all four conflicts at once.

We know intellectually that one day we will *die*. We exist now, but one day we shall cease to be. However, it takes an outer event for most people to make this an emotional reality. In our daily lives we behave as if we are inviolable. This is, of course, useful, as we would not be able to function in our daily lives if we were always aware that we might die at any moment.

Most of us also claim that we value *freedom*, and yet arrange our lives within a set of relatively narrow boundaries.

We also know that we are born alone and that we shall die alone. However close our relations to other people, we are existentially alone. This is a painful fact, and most of us avoid facing it as long as possible. It is frightening to face the *existential isolation*.

Yalom's fourth concept is *meaninglessness*. Life does not have a simple meaning, which all humans share. Each person must face a sense of emptiness and meaninglessness in their life, and emerge with a personal solution.

'The confrontations with the givens of existence are painful, but ultimately healing', Yalom states. In our experience, this is never demonstrated more dramatically than in the grieving over a major loss. When an individual has lost his child or spouse, his eyesight or his hearing or his general health, or when he is confronted with a serious diagnosis like cancer or AIDS, there is no way to escape these four dilemmas unless the mourning is altogether avoided.

Losing a person to whom one is closely connected or losing one's health is like losing part of oneself. The individual can no longer maintain the illusion of being inviolable nor believe in an omnipotent rescuer. This is very frightening. Many ask 'Why me? Why should this happen to me?' In their struggle to find an answer to this question, they face their own mortality and the apparent meaninglessness of life. They must each find a personal solution to be able to engage in life again. This is hard work, and it must be done at a time when the mourner has very little free energy to invest. It is paradoxical that the process of life makes the strongest demand on the individual at the time when he feels most exhausted and overwhelmed.

The mourner needs sympathetic friends and relatives around him to support his grieving, and yet even in the most optimal situation, the griever feels at times his existential isolation perhaps stronger than ever. It is *he* who has lost 'part of himself', not his friends or family. It is *he* who experiences these overwhelming feelings of pain, anger, perhaps guilt and shame, not them. He knows that he has to endure this process – it is hoped with support, but ultimately alone.

And as if all these trials and tribulations were not enough, the mourner finally has to face freedom. As he can no longer believe in his own inviolability or an ultimate rescuer, and having faced his separateness from all other beings, he must take upon himself that he is ultimately responsible for his own life and that the choices he makes shape his destiny.

This is another way of explaining why the process of grieving is a turning-point for better or for worse in the life of any human being. The Danish author Isak Dinesen says it this way in *Out of Africa*, when she quotes the former Swiss national anthem: 'Frei lebt wer sterben kann' ('He who is prepared to die is free').

Chapter two

The four tasks of grief work

When working with grief therapy and crisis intervention, there are many advantages in using a model which divides normal grief work into tasks. The bereaved person must accomplish these tasks if he is to find himself again and perhaps emerge strengthened from his grief. This model accords well with Freud's idea that grief is emotional work that is necessary for healing the wounds which the loss has caused. This not only takes time, it also requires energy and courage. For time does not heal all wounds. By using the expressions 'tasks' and 'grief work' we are emphasizing that an active effort is required to get through this painful process. If this work is inhibited, the grief cannot be resolved, and so develops pathologically.

The drawback of systematizing complicated emotional processes is that there is a risk of simplifying so much that the result is too cut-and-dried and therefore unusable. So it is important to realize that we are working on all the tasks at different levels throughout the course of the grief. In practice, part of normal grief work may look like this. *The first task, accepting that the loss is a reality,* is done on the intellectual level when we realize that our sick spouse, who has been ill for a long time, is dead. In connection with this, we accomplish *the second task: entering into the emotions of grief* on a relatively shallow level as we weep a little on hearing the news. Then we move to *the third task,* that of *acquiring new skills,* when we overcome our uncertainty about new people by getting in touch with the clergyman and the undertaker.

Thus the first three tasks have been accomplished on a fairly simple level. Hours, days or weeks later, it may come home to us that our spouse will never again lie beside us in bed. We shall have to live without body warmth and sexuality. Now we are accomplishing the first task on a deeper level and coming to grips with this partial loss. If we weep over the loss of body warmth and sexuality, we are working on the second task. We are dealing with the third task if we ask a close friend to sleep with us for a while at first. We have now passed through the first, second and third tasks twice on different levels. The next day we perhaps get an invitation to a party and discover a new loss. In future we are going to have to go to parties on our own, perhaps feeling like 'half a couple'. Again we weep with unhappiness and phone up the hosts to tell them, perhaps more openly than usual, that we are not up to being among so many people, because our grief is still so fresh. In this way we have again passed through tasks one, two and three, this time on a new level.

So healthy grief work is a long process in which the first three tasks are done over and over again in various ways. The feelings of pain and sorrow at the loss of body warmth, sexuality, a partner in social life and so on, will thus be repeated again and again. At first, the pain will grow, because the recognition that the loss is irrevocable will slowly become plainer. Also the mourner will often have to overstep his own boundaries and ask for help in ways unknown before.

It will not be until the first three tasks have been repeated a number of times that the grieving person will reach a clarification, making it possible to start on part of *the fourth task*, which is *to reinvest our energy in new ways*. Thus after grieving many times at having to sleep alone, we slowly grow accustomed to it and are at last ready to say a final farewell to body contact with our lost partner. We may be able to begin to enjoy some of the advantages of sleeping alone. The energy that was linked to the loss can thus be released for new life.

It is possible to come to a standstill on all four tasks so that our grief work gets bogged down. On a longer term this may lead to pathological grief. Pathological grief can be divided into three different types: delayed grief, avoided grief and chronic grief.

Delayed or postponed grief

It is not infrequent for people not to react immediately following the events which should evoke grief. They hold on to themselves, they are going to manage, they live for the children who 'mustn't notice anything'. They make sure they are constantly on the go, that they 'have to get on with ...'. The restlessness which we have previously mentioned as an expression of grief is here turned into hyper-activity which keeps the pain at a little distance.*

Here, the first task has been done purely intellectually, but the bereaved person has not got started on the second task at a deeper level. He may indeed have wept a little at the funeral and in the time afterwards, but has suppressed the liberating tears and thus the healing forces. The grief has been delayed.

*L. Hillgaard *et al.*, *Sorg og Krise* (Copenhagen: Munksgaard).

Months or years later, a holiday without responsibilities, a sad film or a fresh grief may reopen the suppressed grief work. If this opening does not come in the course of a few months after the bereavement, there is usually a need for crisis intervention.

Avoided grief

Back in 1937 the psychoanalyst Helene Deutsch described avoided grief. She established that if a bereaved person does not fully express the feelings of grief, this will result in symptoms of various kinds. It is depressing that fifty years later not many professional therapists are yet aware of the many physical and psychological symptoms which can be traced to avoided grief.

Psychosomatic symptoms: Vague pains for which organic cause cannot be found. Actual ailments like peptic ulcers, heart conditions, asthma, headaches and so on. Sometimes the bereaved will develop symptoms that resemble the illness of the deceased.

Psychological symptoms: One often sees a neurotic picture, with sadness, emptiness, anxiety and vehement self-reproaches. There may be strong dependence upon others or the reverse: isolation. Some people may develop phobic behaviour towards anything that might remind them of the deceased. The home is stripped of photographs of the dead one, and the deceased's possessions are removed from it. The cemetery is avoided. Suicide attempts and suicide may occur.

If years later, such a person is exposed to yet another loss by, for instance, being deserted by a fiancé, sometimes a quite different and far more dramatic picture may be seen. The person then enters a crisis which seems out of all proportion. All their thoughts concern the fiancé and the chances of getting him back. Here, too, serious thoughts of suicide may occur, because being alone is so frightening. The person can rarely understand his own violent reaction. Closer analysis then reveals the avoided grief. It is often for a dead parent. We have seen examples of this loss being as much as forty years earlier.

In the literature avoided grief is also called unreleased, repressed, pathological or disguised grief. In cases of avoided grief, grief therapy is necessary.

Chronic grief

In some bereaved people, thoughts about the dead person and the emotions of grief fill their lives to replace almost everything else. Three, six, nine months after the death, the mourner may scarcely think or speak about anything but the loss. The person weeps a good deal, but without really giving way to a deep flow of tears. Work on the first and second tasks is thus going on, but on a superficial level, and the person has primarily come to a standstill on the third task, that of acquiring new skills so that life can have value without the deceased. It is characteristic that these people reject the idea that a final farewell to the deceased is necessary. The fourth task is being denied.

Unlike the person who avoids grief, the chronic griever will almost worship everything that has to do with the lost one. The deceased's bedroom may remain untouched for years, their clothes may still hang in the wardrobe, and there are often pictures of the deceased everywhere. The chronic griever frequently visits the cemetery.

However, it may also happen that the chronic griever develops phobic behaviour, like that seen in avoided grief. She avoids the joint bedroom or keeps away from memory-filled places so as not to trigger off deep pain.

When, years after the death, it is still hardly possible to talk of anything but the deceased, a person's network of friends is soon used up. So it often happens that people in chronic grief isolate themselves and become bitter and unapproachable in their pain-filled everyday life.

It is our view that, in chronic grief, grief therapy may be effective in the first year or two after the loss, before the pattern has become fixed and set. After that, more lengthy individual psychotherapy will be necessary.

The wound left in the mind by the loss or trauma may become inflamed in three different ways. The healing grief work may be delayed: on the first or second task the bereaved person remains at a level which is relatively easy to reach by means of crisis intervention. In the case of avoided grief, it is usually the second task through which the client needs to be helped and this requires an offer of grief therapy. Chronic grief is identified when the grieving person is unable or unwilling to acquire new skills. The grieving person thus comes to a standstill on the third task, but also has problems with the second task. The bereaved person enters into the emotions of grief, but in such a rigid manner that they are not released. In all three cases the fourth task is excluded. The griever cannot reinvest energy in other people.

In the following, we shall review the four tasks so thoroughly that therapists will be able to identify the point at which the bereaved has come to a standstill, and obtain some idea of how it is possible to help her to get started on the tasks, so that her grief work may be finished.

The first task: acceptance of the loss

The first task of the mourner is to accept the reality of the loss. We have found it practical to divide this recognition into two phases. First comes the intellectual realization of the loss, and then the emotional realization, which is on a deeper level and contains the recognition that the loss is irrevocable. This is the beginning of the fourth task.

In normal, healthy grief work these two phases may coincide or follow each other rapidly. As a therapist, one may meet clients who have come to a halt in both the first and the second of the phases.

The first phase: intellectual recognition

As a rule the first phase does not cause any difficulties when the loss has been foreseen for a long time, as with a death after lengthy illness, or a spouse moving away after a separation which has been prepared for. But in cases of sudden or violent events a person may receive a shock. They may then react by denying that the event has occurred, may laugh aloud or in some other way distance themselves from the situation.

The shock and the denial are the mind's healthy defence against being overwhelmed by reality. It gives the person an opportunity to open up slowly to the reality of the loss. These reactions may last from minutes to a couple of days, until the reality dawns upon the person. If it takes longer, then crisis intervention is normally necessary.

In rare cases, people may react with an acute psychotic state, because the realities of the situation are so overwhelming that they cannot accommodate them.

One example is a woman who ran over a young girl with her car. She drove on, and on the way home developed a reactive psychotic state. On arriving home to her husband, she did not know what day it was or where she was. Nor did she know what had happened in the last couple of hours and talked incoherently. Her husband immediately arranged for her to go into a psychiatric ward. Here she was at first treated with anti-psychotic medication until, after twenty-four hours, the worst confusion had subsided. Then she wished to remember what had happened. For many hours at a time a nurse sat with her and helped her by supporting the memories that floated up with what the nurse herself had heard. After some days she remembered most of it and was no longer psychotic. Then she needed ordinary crisis intervention in order to cope with her feelings and the consequences of her actions.

The first phase of the task has been completed when the bereaved person can confirm without hesitation that the death has occurred.

The second phase: deeper recognition that the loss is irrevocable

When someone dies, it takes time for it to sink into the minds of their kith and kin that the person has gone for ever. They will never again see the dead one, hear the well-known voice and feel contact with them. They will no longer have a future together.

Many mourners have a need to recount over and over again the details of the circumstances of the death in order to support themselves in this difficult acceptance. Here, patient listening is a great help.

An old man of our acquaintance lost his wife after fifty years of marriage. We had supported him at the hospital and saw him both shortly before and just after this wife died. For months afterwards he told us the whole course of the illness with all its small occurrences every time we met him, even though we had been there ourselves. We listened every time, because we knew how necessary this process was for him. Slowly he worked his way to an acceptance that his wife was dead and gone for ever.

In the first long period after the death it is usual for a mourner to alternate between believing that she can hear the dead one's step on the stairs and then recalling that he is dead. An hour later the telephone rings and she catches herself thinking that the hospital is phoning to say that it was someone else who had died. In this way the mind is at work absorbing the realities little by little.

In this healthy process, many people, in the first period, see the deceased in his usual chair in front of the television or they hear the dead person's voice. For a long time after the death, they may believe that they can see the dead person in the street, only to discover after a closer look that it was the colour of the coat, the hairstyle, or the gait, that had set off their imagination. In the normal process the bereaved thus alternate between periods when the reality is denied (they see the dead person) and periods when the reality is clear to them (they feel the loss).

There are great differences in the way in which bereaved people deal with pictures and objects that have belonged to the deceased. This will often give a first clue to whether the grief process is going to take a healthy or pathological course. The healthy grief process is characterized by being flexible. The process which may develop pathologically is more rigid. It will be often possible to see this quite concretely in the way the bereaved person relates to the deceased's possessions.

It is normal to leave the dead person's bedroom untouched for a time after the death. How does the bereaved person use this room? Does he go in there from time to time to make contact with the memories and perhaps get a warming feeling of the dead one's presence? Or does he spend many hours in there every day while in his imagination arranging it as a memorial room? Or perhaps he does the reverse: gives the room a wide berth as if it were not part of the home? The last two possibilities are both rigid and suggest a risk of chronic and avoided grief respectively.

Some people empty the home of the dead one's things fairly quickly. Is it done over a period or all at once? Are all the photographs put up in the loft, or is there a picture of the dead one on show? Does the bereaved person keep the person's favourite pipe, her ring, or the child's teddy-bear – or is everything thrown out? If a person keeps something, it shows that they are capable of both holding on to the memories and facing reality. But if everything has to go, that reveals an emotional rigidity which may inhibit the work of grieving.

Both the person who clings on to the things and the one who throws everything out are, in a way, trying to go on living as though nothing has happened. It is characteristic of the former group that they spend a disproportionate amount of their time dwelling upon the circumstances of the death. The guilt they might themselves have, the blame accorded to others (doctors, drivers or others), the possibilities of calling these people to account, and so on.

The second group is more inclined to play down the loss: 'Life must go on', 'We'll cope', and so forth. These people come to a standstill in their grief work and seldom get started on the deep necessary emotions of which the second task consists.

Should one see the dead person?

In the last century, most people died at home with their families, and it was natural for the corpse to remain at home for a while so that the relatives had time to pay their respects. This encounter with the stiff, cold, lifeless body made the loss plainer and eased the recognition that the dead person had gone for ever. As it gradually became more customary to die in hospital, the ritual of viewing the corpse became less usual. There seems nowadays to be a tendency to revive this custom. In most people the distressing sight triggers off a reaction of grief, because it is made clear that a farewell is inevitable. The controls come down and they begin to weep.

We would like to stress how important it is to see the dead person. In our work we have often seen how much more difficult the parting becomes if a person has last seen the dead person alive. It becomes even more difficult if the body is never found, as may happen in drownings, air crashes, natural disasters, in war and so on. It may then be almost impossible to let go of the hope that the missing person may be alive somewhere.

Sometimes the dead person may be much altered or even repulsive to look at – after a traffic accident or a fire or such-like – and then it must be weighed up once more whether it would be a good thing to see the corpse. As a rule the decisive factor is whether there can be relatives or other people present who are able to cope with the mourner's tears, anger or fear.

A mother was referred to us shortly after her two children had been killed. In this case, through enquiries to the Institute of Forensic Medicine, we made sure that the children were not a distressing sight. There, as is always done, they put in a lot of work to make the children look as nice as possible. The mother saw the children accompanied by her closest kin. Both the mother and we consider that this confrontation was crucial for her grief work getting off to a natural start.

If, as a therapist, one is in doubt whether to recommend that the bereaved person sees the corpse, it is possible to get information about the appearance of the deceased from the hospital or undertaker.

Adults who as children lost a parent and did not see the corpse nearly always feel that they were cheated of something important in not having said their final farewell to their mother or father. It is therefore important not to forget to take the children with you to see the corpse. You have to prepare them for what they will be seeing, and must be ready to cope with their reactions and answer their questions afterwards. A number of adults who grew up in the country have told us how they recall taking leave of their dead grandparents in the parlour with candles and their hand firmly in that of mother or father as a good shared experience. In this way the children are given an understanding that death is a natural conclusion to life and it becomes less frightening. It is also important to include children at the funeral. They should be told what will happen at the ceremony and that they will see many grown-ups crying and that this is natural. Here too it is important for there to be grown-ups present to support the children during and after the funeral.

Stillborn babies

In hospitals there has always been great uncertainty about stillborn babies. In England for the last ten years they have been working on teaching the staff how they can support the parents in seeing the dead baby. The parents have not of course seen the child alive, but during the pregnancy they have felt it in the womb. They have attached dreams and imaginings to the expected child. The parents' grief work is inhibited if they are allowed to leave the hospital without being given the chance of seeing the baby. It may be a great support to the parents to know as many details as possible about the baby that they have lost. If they see the baby, they may know that they have lost a little girl with dark hair and features resembling one of them. This helps to make the grief more concrete. If parents see their dead baby and bury it, they are, as a rule, well started on the work of grieving.

This group of parents was formerly neglected in Denmark, but fortunately here too a positive development is taking place, so that more and more parents are being supported by the staff in seeing the baby.

When the loss is not accepted

In the following we shall touch on two concrete examples of how crisis intervention can operate when the loss is not accepted. This method is usually used when the person afflicted by crisis or bereavement is unable to begin on the first task.

The first example is a woman whose husband had left her. In a divorce the loss may be at least as stressful as a death. The first task is particularly difficult when the spouse is not dead. Even when there are clear and unambiguous signals that the relationship is definitively over, it may be hard to abandon all hope of getting one's spouse back when he or she is still in the neighbourhood.

Pat, aged 35, was referred to us three months after her husband Frank had suddenly left her. They had been married for twelve years, and she thought that the marriage had been good. There were two children. It came as a shock to her when without warning Frank moved in with another woman and declared that their marriage was over. He repeated this on the few occasions when she saw him afterwards.

For a while after this she lived in a state of unreality. At work she moved around like a sleepwalker and pretended that every-thing was normal at home. She looked after the children as usual. It was as if she was soon expecting Frank to come home from a long journey. After three months had passed, Frank demanded that Pat should go to a solicitor with a view to a divorce. The lawyer was the first person whom she told that Frank had left her. The lawyer was concerned that Pat would not face up to her divorce and referred her to us. Pat must also have felt that she needed help, for she agreed to meet us.

Crisis intervention

The first aim of the treatment was to break down Pat's massive denial of reality. First, the method was to ask Pat to give a detailed account of the day on which Frank had left her and the time just afterwards. This was hard for her, because she was ashamed at having been deserted. We asked many questions. What had happened when Frank said he was going to move out? What had she said? What had she thought about afterwards? Were the children there? Did he say where he was going? What did she think afterwards? What did she do? We pressed her to give as clear a picture as possible of the traumatic situation, but we did not try to get her in contact with her emotions.

The next step was to get her to repeat some sentences which confronted her with the fact that she was going to be divorced. We asked her to say: 'I have been deserted', 'I am going to be divorced' and 'I am a single parent now'. These sentences expressed the loss unambiguously. The first couple of times she repeated the sentences mechanically under our pressure. After three months of effort to keep the acceptance of the loss away from her consciousness, it was an exhausting effort just to repeat these three sentences three or four times. The therapist may appear brutal, because she is so directive and confrontational, but this is necessary. Pat took a long time to conquer herself and say these sentences. She looked stiffly at the floor while she spoke.

The next step of the crisis intervention was to support her into contact with someone else. She needed help to be aware that someone else was seeing and hearing her while she repeated the distressing sentences that faced her with the reality of the situation. This part of the process is important, because contact makes reality less frightening. If we had worked individually with Pat, we would have asked her to look at us while she repeated the three sentences. But we were working in a group and therefore asked her to choose one of the other members of the group.

Pat took a long time to choose whom she would contact. At first she did not dare to look at the person she chose, but with our support she quite slowly raised her head and met his eyes. Thus we made sure there was eye contact before she articulated: I have been deserted. I am going to be divorced. I am a single parent. Now Pat had told someone else about her misfortune and had thus taken her next important step towards recognizing it herself. This shy and emotionally inhibited woman had at the same time discovered that it may be necessary for someone to overstep their own bounds to make constructive use of a network.

In Pat's case the rest of the treatment was rapid. By the next group meeting she began to weep copiously when we asked her to repeat the same emotionally charged sentences. She had now got over her first fright at the strong feelings and felt very relieved. Pat had escaped from the feeling of unreality and was started on the necessary pain, the second task. Just a week later she came along to the group with aching arms after spending many hours sawing the double bed in two in a savage rage. She managed to tell her colleagues about her divorce and used them and some women friends as a network. One day she came to the group without her wedding ring.

Pat came to the group eleven times over nearly three months. Part of the farewell letter she wrote to the group runs like this:

When I started in the group, I was living in a kind of unreal state of mind. Things happened around me, but sort of didn't penetrate my awareness. What got me out of this shock phase was a combination of several things. First, the group .... Today I am in the position of feeling very good, having got a big chance in life by being able to start over again with a mass of experiences, and having some really good friends who have patiently listened to me and have come when I needed them – and I do not feel that I owe them anything at all. I do not need to change myself. I have learnt to use the people I have. I have learnt a good deal about myself; for example, that I also contain feelings like grief, anger and vengefulness.

Twenty-eight-year-old Anne was referred to us six months after her fiancé John's sudden death due to an accident at work. She felt sad and empty. She had not wept and all day she carried on an interior dialogue with John. Intellectually she knew that John was dead, but all the same she expected him to be in the flat when she came home. She soothed herself with anxiety-relieving medicine and sleeping tablets.

We asked her to describe her last hours with John. She related that she had been sitting with him when he died. When he was dead, she had got up without talking to anyone and had gone straight home. What had their last contact been like? Had John known that he was going to die? Had they talked about it? Had his parents been there? What had he looked like when he died? Had she been prepared for it to happen that evening? Had she been afraid? Had she touched him or said anything to him after he was dead? Anne answered the questions slowly and hesitantly in a flat, dreary voice.

We asked her to go home and write about John's death, if possible with even more details. We also asked her to contact two friends and ask them to listen to her description of her last hours with John. She could tell them in her own words or read aloud what she had written.

The next time she came she told us that it had been a good experience to write about the difficult period which she had been trying to forget. She had talked to two friends but had not cried. This time we asked her to tell about the funeral and the time afterwards in the same detailed way. She suggested on her own that she would write it down and tell the same two friends about it. She had still not cried and her feeling of unreality was almost unchanged.

When she came next time, her dog had died, and on our expressing sympathy at how much of her childhood security had gone with it, she was able to start crying about it. One of us said, 'It is dead, like John, it will never come back again. Just as you will never be seeing John again.' She replied, 'You mustn't say that, it is much too cruel', and put her hands over her ears. 'It is very, very sad, but it is true, and I must say it. John is dead and you will never be seeing him again. You have lost him.' And then the deep, liberating weeping came from deep down inside her, and one of us sat close beside her, repeating now and again, 'It is very hard for you. John is dead and what you had together is over. You will never be seeing him again.' And each time the sentence evoked a vague protest and more deep weeping. Finally the weeping died away, and the client was wrapped in a blanket and lay in the group while we carried on. The grief reaction had been triggered off.

When somebody needs help with their grief work we have to identify the task on which she has come to a halt and plan our interventions on that basis. It was fairly easy to see that neither Pat nor Anne had got as far as accepting that they had to bid farewell to their husband and fiancé. We therefore chose a confrontational technique that led them into the pain of facing up to their loss.

As we have said, work on the various tasks does interweave. It is thus not unusual for a bereaved person to have gained some intellectual understanding of his or her loss and therefore to have begun to weep, yet without having achieved a deeper realization that the loss is irrevocable.

When applying crisis intervention in grief therapy the timing is all-important. If the therapist starts out from an assessment that the client is to be helped to go deeper into the necessary pain (the second task), whereas the client will not yet accept that the loss is final (the first task), the client will not feel that he is being understood by the therapist. There is therefore a risk that the client will break off the treatment.

A wrong assessment of the first task

Forty-year-old Peter was referred to us four months after his teenage son had died from a sudden illness. Peter had been very close to his son, and the boy's death had been a great shock. In the preliminary conversation he seemed dreary and resigned and wept the whole time. He had many thoughts of suicide.

In the group he cried most of the time. We were misled by his many tears into believing that he had completed the first task and was well on the way with the second. We considered that he needed support to enter into the deep pain of bidding farewell to his son. At his third meeting in the group we therefore elected to focus on his taking leave of his son. We said that he now had to face up to the fact that he had to begin the difficult process of saying goodbye to his son. We mentioned how sad it was that he would never see his son again. His reaction showed that our timing was wrong. He protested and said that *it would never be possible*. We repeated our confrontation without realizing that Peter had not yet accomplished the first task, because he would still not accept that the loss was irrevocable. Our confrontation merely reinforced his defences against facing up to this.

After this meeting, Peter stayed away. We contacted him a number of times on the phone, and he promised to come, but stayed away. Instead, he intensified his campaign in the press to get the hospital to take responsibility for wrong treatment of his son. We knew that he had many phantasies about killing the doctor responsible. His battle with the medical system was primarily a defence against ever accepting that his son was dead. As long as he could fight, his son was in a way still with him. The weeping which we believed was part of the necessary pain was presumably what has been described in Chapter One as 'calling weeping' for the dead one.

If we had realized Peter's problems at an earlier point, we might have made a different plan. We would not have pressed him with the word 'farewell'. We would have left him to sit in the group, in which he felt secure, and allowed him to listen to how the others were working through the first and second tasks in their loss. We might have requested him just to articulate to someone else in the group that his son was dead. In this way he would slowly be able to approach the acceptance of the irrevocable nature of the loss. We have good experience of allowing the group's emotional intensity and security, in a gentle way, to help people with great resistance to the work of grieving through the first difficult acceptance of realities.

We regard Peter as seriously threatened if nobody can help him to go further in the work of grieving. Peter's feeling of hopelessness and his thoughts of suicide will not disappear by themselves. He risks developing a chronic state of grief. In the longer term one may fear an illness picture resembling depression. It is also possible that he will get psychosomatic symptoms and, in the worst case, become seriously ill.

The second task: the emotions of grief

We have called this book *Healing Pain*, because the work of the second task is the central feature both in crisis intervention and in grief therapy. This section deals with the various emotions of grief, and how people are helped to accommodate them.

The manifold nature of grief has found brilliant expression in literature, art and music. In the literature on grief authors frequently quote from the world of art to depict what is often a violent and frightening process. 'It was as if a bomb had gone off inside me and somebody was poking at the wounds with a needle', wrote one of our clients. The bereaved person is full of despair, fear, feelings of being abandoned, loneliness and perhaps guilt and shame. There may also be violent anger: anger against the world, against fate, against God or against the deceased. The person's soul has been shaken.

The normal grief process

The course of grief is remarkably uniform, considering how much we differ in other ways. In the normal course of grief, the emotions change a lot. During the course of a single day someone may feel a sharp physical pain at one time, a deep sense of loss accompanied by profound sobbing at another, a nagging sense of guilt an hour later, and then anger: 'How could he die and leave me?' Between these strong emotions there may have been periods of relative calm. Over time these emotions help to cleanse and heal the wound. In healthy grief work it is this flexibility that gives the mourner the opportunity to enter into his deeper feelings at certain times and to get a little peace at others, thus gathering strength for the next round. The grieving person thus goes in and out of the emotions of grief. It is a hard and exhausting process.

As time goes on, there are longer and longer intervals between the difficult periods, and their intensity wanes. Finally they fade away completely. Left behind is a yearning pain which particularly makes itself felt at anniversaries and festive seasons. In the case of a serious bereavement, it is a process that may take several years.

Pathological grief development

The great majority of the 600 or so people we have worked with in the grief group had come to a halt mainly on the second task. Their emotions were not being given expression and so the healing process was being hampered.

In any bereavement there are many component losses. If our spouse dies, we may also have lost a breadwinner, a confidant, a lover, the mother or father of our child, a helper with the housework and so on. Linked to each of these areas are memories and voids, tears and perhaps anger. It is part of the healthy, flexible grief process to deal emotionally with each of these bereavements. The task of the therapist in grief support and grief therapy is to help the client to identify the component losses and express the emotions linked to them.

Profound grief and profound sobbing belong together. Weeping has a therapeutic effect. Not all mourners seem to need to feel anger, but if the anger does come, it too can be part of the healing process. Guilt, shame, fear, jealousy and relief all enter into the normal work of grieving and must also have their place. Many of these emotions seem contradictory to the client. The task of the therapist is to help the client to accept that we all have contradictory feelings towards those we are fond of, and that anger does not exclude a sense of loss and loving feelings.

In our society, strong emotions have a frightening effect on many people, and that is why working with the emotions of grief presents difficulties for many therapists. So in the following we shall review in a very down-to-earth way some methods and principles that are used in helping people to get started on the second task.

Grief therapy when the emotions of grief have to be released

Sandra, aged 26, was referred to us because of giddiness, nausea, the fear of fainting and intense anger against older women in general.

Sandra's mother had died ... months previously after a brief illness. She had been her 'best friend' and they had talked together every day. She felt that her mother had supported her in everything. Right from childhood she had been afraid of losing her mother. In other words, there was a strong mutual dependency between mother and daughter.

Sandra had completed the first phase of the first task, having accepted intellectually that her mother was dead. She had scarcely wept at all. She could not imagine that it would be possible for her to go on living without her mother.

Sandra's giddiness and anxiety showed us that she was spending too much strength on keeping the necessary pain at bay. We assumed that the loss of her mother appeared to her so great that she was afraid of being overwhelmed by a sense of chaos if she let go and felt the loss.

All this information came out in the preliminary interview. At the close of it Sandra was offered a place in a grief group. She was told that on the first occasion she needed only to attend and observe what went on. Then she could decide for herself if she wanted to continue in the group.

The first meeting

At the first meeting Sandra was exposed to intense emotional influence. She saw several people weeping copiously; she saw and heard someone giving vent to his anger with the hospital system, and someone who said goodbye to the group after successful treatment. So she was confronted with the emotions of grief in various ways. The farewell to the client who had completed his treatment in the group gave her insight into the growth that is possible for someone who dares to give way to their emotions. This helped to give her *hope*.

Five minutes before the meeting ended, we asked how she had liked being in the group. She seemed a little scared at the intensity, and we spent some minutes making sure that she would come again. Then at our request she told the others in the group that she was having to work on her mother's death. We made sure that she would stay after the meeting and have a cup of coffee with the others, as we know that this gives an added sense of security to new group members.

The second meeting

At their second meeting we nearly always get the clients to relate the circumstances around their bereavement. Sandra went into details about her mother's brief illness and told of her fear of accepting that her mother was dying. Her mother had told her that she was dying, but Sandra had not heeded her. Sandra had not felt up to staying by her mother when she died but had run out of the sick-room in fear of fainting. She had been given the chance of seeing her mother's corpse, but had refused.

Sandra's dominant feeling was guilt. In clients with a need for grief therapy we often find that the sense of guilt is less frightening than the sense of bereavement. When feeling our loss, we are confronted with the parting. As long as we continue to dwell upon what we might have done differently, we have not yet completely abandoned hope that the death may be reversible.

So our first goal was to reduce her sense of guilt. The method used was to give her the opportunity to return in imagination to her mother's death-bed and to help her to do something different from what she actually had done. We wanted to help her to be confronted again by her mother's death and this time to be able to begin to say farewell to her mother.

We explained to Sandra that she had been in a state of shock when her mother died because it had happened so suddenly. She had needed time to grow accustomed to the idea that her mother was going to die. She had therefore shielded herself in a healthy way by leaving her mother. But now eight months had passed, and here in the group with the rest of us to support her, she would be able to act differently from the way she had at the time. We therefore proposed to her that in her imagination she should work on her mother's death-bed, and she agreed to this.

One of us sat close to her to give her strength. Her respiration was rapid and shallow. We asked her to breathe out slowly. We breathed out slowly ourselves to show what we meant. After breathing out slowly a couple of times, we asked her to breathe slowly through her mouth. Then her respiration became slower and deeper.

We asked her to close her eyes. Slowly and calmly we told her to see again the hospital ward with its yellow curtains which she had previously described to us. We asked her to see her mother in bed and go up to the bed. This time she was to remain in the room until her mother had died. She was to tell her mother everything she ought to know before she died. Sandra sat for a long time (three or four minutes) with the tears running down her cheeks. Finally she told her mother that she loved her and wanted to say goodbye. Her weeping became even deeper, and she was sobbing like the helpless child she at that moment felt herself to be. We sat her beside one of our trainees, who put her arms round her as one does to a little child. There she could sit and weep as long as she wanted, with the tender care which the trainee's warm body gave her. She could now allow herself to feel the loss which she had been keeping at bay for eight months.

The third meeting

Sandra told the group that from time to time she had begun to cry at home with her sister, but it still seemed strange and unusual to her to do this. After that, she stayed away for a long time. Phone calls showed that first she was ill for a bit, later she had some work problems to which she felt she had to give greater priority than the grief work.

Four months later

When her problems at work had been more or less settled, we applied some pressure and got her to come to the group four times in a row. The first time after the long break we noticed that she cried quite freely when others in the group were working on their grief. She also cried a lot when she told us that she still missed her mother.

At the second session we gave her an assignment aimed at improving her use of the network (the third task). She was to tell her father how much she missed her mother and not hide her tears from him. She agreed to the assignment. At the third session she told us that it had taken some mustering of courage to open up to her father like that, but she had managed it, and it had been a good experience.

We became aware that Sandra still had considerable guilt feelings towards her mother. We therefore requested her to write a letter to her mother telling her what a traumatic experience her illness and death had been for her. She was to place her mother's picture in front of her (it turned out to have been hidden away) and make sure she had plenty of time and tranquillity while she did it. If her emotions made themselves felt, she was not to keep them back but give them free rein. If she became afraid, she was to contact her sister, who was her closest confidante.

As arranged, Sandra brought her letter with her to the fourth meeting. While we chatted about what it had felt like to write the letter, her mother's picture was passed round the group, so we all got a sight of it. After that, it was laid in front of Sandra, who in tears read the letter aloud to her mother:

> On the day you had to go to hospital I was with you; it was so horrible, I was trembling with fear and did not dare to be there. I have never seen you so ill, weak, and limp, sweating and panting .... After Dad had told us the diagnosis I didn't cry, I felt completely empty and turned to stone. It was not till two days later that I plucked up courage to visit you. The first day you asked: Are all of you there? Yes, Mum, one, two and three. The apparatus began to bleep, and your forehead was icy with sweat, your skin was quite grey. I wailed like one possessed that you'd got to stay with us and things went black before my eyes, and my legs began to wobble. Dad put his arm round me, and you said in a small, almost apologetic voice: 'Well, I am still here – but not for very long'. That was the last thing you said in your life.... Later I kissed you and said goodbye to you and that I loved you and would never forget you. You didn't respond, but I think you heard me. I couldn't stand being there waiting for you to die, but I couldn't go either – I was being tugged both ways.... But I went, I went away and left you, Mum. You died in the night.... I have never before been able to imagine how terrible it is to lose someone you love – what a crater it leaves behind. It was as if a bomb had gone off inside me, and there was someone with a needle poking at my wounds. It hurts terribly, Mum – but you know that; you had never properly got over Granny's death – and it changes one so much. I can't think, feel or remember – and my legs often haven't wanted to move from the spot. But I can walk now, Mum, and I know it's your wish for me that your death won't stop me living and using my life. And I do feel now that, at each step I take, there is hope ahead. I love you.

We asked her to repeat the emotionally most provocative sentence: 'But I went, I went away and left you, Mum'. This made the weeping deeper, so that it passed over into sobbing.

After this meeting Sandra stayed away again for some months. Finally, she came twice running, at our request, to complete the group treatment.

The last time she came with a farewell letter to the grief group. She mentioned how she felt after reading out the letter to her mother:

> It's both agreeable and frightening to be here. Frightening because you overstep boundaries, expose your innermost feelings. The feelings that are expressed here would not come out under any other circumstances, and actually one would like to forget them. Agreeable, because when you've got rid of these feelings, it's like flying. An incredible relief has come over me, it has taught me much, I dare to do more now....

Factors in deciding on treatment

In grief therapy we work with a clear focus on the grief reaction. The goal of grief therapy is to help the client complete the first three tasks and, if possible, to get a good way into the fourth task. At the preliminary interview we therefore have to make an assessment of whether the things the client complains of reflect a pathological development of grief. Selecting the line of treatment is a subject we shall deal with more fully in Chapter Three. Here we shall merely take a look at how it was done in Sandra's case.

At the preliminary interview, Sandra complained of giddiness, nausea, the fear of fainting and intense anger against older women. For many years she had been of an anxious disposition, but these troublesome symptoms had not appeared until her mother died. Besides these symptoms she was also having some difficulties in getting on with other people at her work. These problems had been going on for some years. It was our assessment that Sandra's lack of self-reliance was the reason behind both the pathological development of her grief and the problems at her place of work. As the actual symptoms had not occurred until after her mother's death, her separation from her mother must be a crucial factor. We assumed that if she could begin to deal with that – that is, to start on her grief work – then the problems at her work place would also change in character. These were the reasons for our offering Sandra grief therapy rather than any other treatment.

Methods and principles of grief therapy

In the following we want to comment upon the methods we used to help Sandra to begin on the second task. This section is also a review of the most important guidelines in grief therapy and consists of the following sub-sections:

Planning interventions
Getting the client to 'tell the story' in detail

How to penetrate into the pain and sense of loss
Releasing tears
Body contact with the clients

Anger, bitterness, guilt and shame are also parts of the second task:

Anger
Anger with the deceased, God or fate
Working on anger
Unfinished anger
Bitterness
Guilt
Shame

Other component methods in grief therapy including the use of:

Pictures, objects and music
Letter-writing

Planning interventions

The therapist is active and directive in grief therapy. Almost all the time she is focusing on the course of the grief. She plans each intervention from an assessment of where the client has got to in his grief work. Is the intervention aimed at the first task and so should face the client with his loss? Is it intended to try to lead the client deeper into an emotion? If so, what emotion? If that is the aim, which emotion is assessed as being closest to the surface? If it is the sense of bereavement, does the client need to weep, perhaps to learn to sob? Or does the pressure come from anger? If so, how are we to help the client express it? Should we support the client in visualizing the deceased in front of him and giving vent to his anger? Or should we suggest that the client writes a letter to the deceased about his anger? Or should we encourage the client to write to the doctor who perhaps let him down or visit him to express his dissatisfaction? All the time the therapist has to make choices based on her assessment of where the client has got to in the process.

It may be, as in Sandra's case, a sense of guilt which 'blocks out' the sense of loss and the pain. Sometimes shame is the dominant emotion – shame that one's son has committed suicide or shame at having become a widow. If so, the therapist must begin by getting the client to express his shame.

Getting the client to 'tell the story' in detail

Everyone has a natural need to talk about a stressful experience. The experience may be compared to a burden. The more details we get the chance to tell, the more we have unburdened ourselves. In a major trauma, we often have to relate our experience many times to get rid of the burden.

We commence practically all courses of grief therapy by asking our clients to recount the loss in all its details. That gives an excellent basis for analysing where the client has got stuck and for planning the first interventions from there.

For some time Sandra had been keeping at bay the inner pictures and the emotions surrounding her mother's illness and death. It was emotionally very disturbing for her to recall the course of events. We asked many searching questions and expressed our sympathy, but did nothing to lead her deeper into the emotions. If we had wished, we might (for instance) have asked her to repeat the most difficult passages. We considered that we needed to hear the whole course of events before we could plan our interventions.

How to penetrate into the pain and sense of loss

The great majority of our clients need help in going deeper into weeping. The more the client dares to let go and enter into the pain, the greater is the sense of relief afterwards. So we have to be prepared to make emotionally highly confrontational statements, like 'Karl is dead, you will never be seeing him again, and you will never feel his warm body again'. When one is unused to grief therapy, this may seem cruel. Not until one has many times seen the beneficial effects of being confrontational in this way does it become an integral part of the method of treatment. Of course, the knack is to find the sentence or sentences which strike home. As a rule the client will himself give us ideas of where to strike. For instance, we may listen attentively and observe the client's body language while he is describing the death in detail. Emotional reactions of face and body, altered breathing, unsuitable laughter, pauses and so on reveal which sections of the story are the most provocative. Often it will be enough just to feed back the client's own statements, laying stress on the hard emotions of the story: 'It sounds as if it was *very, very hard* for you to be there *quite alone* with *the children crying* at a time when you yourself were so *upset and unhappy.*' An intervention like that brought a woman to tears. For five months after her husband's sudden death she had been set in a round of hectic activity.

One can also pay attention to what the client leaves out. If the client says, '...and then it was all over', we know that the word *dead* is so emotionally charged that it is being avoided. An intervention might then be: 'What is the *hardest* thing about your mother being *dead* and that you will *never* see her again?'

When Sandra was telling us about her mother's death-bed, she paused for several seconds and swallowed before she told us that she had run out of the sick-room. There were two emotions behind the pause: guilt feelings at having let her mother down, and fear of saying goodbye to her. Prompted by a question from us, she told us that she had not seen her mother dead. This was said with an apologetic smile. Once more she was saying that she was afraid of saying goodbye. We had the choice between working on her feeling of guilt or working on her fear of taking leave of her mother. We chose the feeling of guilt, because it lay closest, and because we had to reduce it in order to be able to penetrate to the sense of bereavement. We might also have used other interventions. We might have said 'How *hard* it must be for you that you had to *let yourself and your mother down* by running out just before she *died*. Which is the worst?' Or, 'Your mother's death-bed sounds very stressful for you. Tell us again, slowly and in detail, what happened and what you felt. What was the *worst* thing?' As mentioned, we did something different again. We sent her imagination back to her mother's death-bed to say the goodbye she was running away from. This intervention worked well, but the other two might have done just as well.

When the aim is to help a client to make contact with his emotions, it is important for the body to co-operate. The therapist must therefore be attentive to the client's body language so as to take note of tensions and breathing. The client must sit at ease in the chair with both feet on the ground. If he sits on the edge of the chair or crosses his legs, he is putting an unnecessary brake on his emotions. Rapid and shallow breathing leads to anxiety and giddiness, but slow, deep breathing in which the diaphragm rises and falls allows more contact with unrestrained emotions. So we always use the very precise directions we gave to Sandra (see page 41) when we wish a client to enter into their weeping or anger.

Releasing tears

The more slowly the client breathes and the deeper his weeping becomes, the more releasing it is. One may use the image that deep weeping cleanses the wound right to the bottom, but shallow crying only cleans the surface.

Sometimes a client says, 'I cried all yesterday evening; I was quite exhausted afterwards, but I don't think I feel much better.' On enquiry it nearly always turns out that the client had just been tearful all the time, instead of giving way to sobs. It is our experience that someone can only sob deeply for ten or twenty minutes, then the weeping dies down by itself. Then he can get a bit of peace and gather strength for the next fit of weeping. If someone only frets tearfully, he can keep it up for hours, even days.

Shallow crying is like the baby's 'calling weeping' when its mother is too far away. The actual relief will not occur until the mother returns.

Like the baby, the grieving person is not much relieved by 'calling weeping'.

In deep sobbing there is an acceptance that all hope of seeing the dead one again is over. The final farewell is inevitable. It may be said that profound weeping contains a letting-go of the dead person. In sobbing, the breathing is done so deep down in the body that many more muscles are affected, and the subsequent relaxation of tension is therefore more profound.

Body contact with the clients

Most therapists feel it natural to put an arm around a client who is crying over a loss. In the great majority of cases this gives a sense of acceptance and sympathy, enabling the client to get closer to the 'letting-go' kind of weeping. This is true of both men and women.

But it is important to remember that, to some clients, body contact has the quite opposite effect. They stiffen and become insecure. They may construe the contact as a sign that they are to stop crying. So in each case one has to be aware how the body contact is working. Sometimes it may be a good idea to ask if it will be all right to take their hand or put an arm round their shoulder. As a rule clients are able to give a clear answer as to what helps and what hinders the process.

When Sandra had said goodbye to her mother in imagination, we sat her close beside a trainee. She sat with her head resting on the trainee's shoulder, like a small child beside its mother. There she continued to weep, because the body contact gave her courage to let go.

Anger, bitterness, guilt and shame are also important parts of the second task.

Anger

A certain amount of anger is part of normal grief work. Bowlby makes a comparison with the small child's anger when its mother goes away from it. When the mother comes back, the child kicks her. It hopes that will make her understand that she mustn't do that again! If a young child is separated from its mother for some time, it goes through what is called a protest phase with violent outbreaks of aggression. Bowlby considers that the anger is to be seen as bonding behaviour like 'calling weeping'. The anger is one of the young child's innate survival mechanisms.

Part of the anger which a grieving person expresses can therefore be understood as a 'holding on to' anger. As long as, rightly or wrongly, someone is able in their mind to blame the doctors, the nurses, the ambulance men for not doing the right thing, then the dead person is, in a way, not quite gone. There is still a magic possibility that what has happened can be changed!

Anger with the deceased, God or fate

It takes a certain amount of courage to direct one's anger at the deceased or at the God who may be responsible for the pain and meaninglessness that the grieving person feels. On a longer term, this anger does seem to give more relief than the 'holding on to' anger, although there may be an element of 'holding on to' in the anger at the dead person.

Themes in the anger with the deceased may be: 'How could you desert me, leaving me with thousands of problems and responsibility for our children?', 'Why didn't you go to the doctor five years ago when I told you to?', 'Why didn't you take more care of yourself so you didn't die of heart failure at fifty?', 'If you weren't dead already, I could kill you for all the pain you've caused me!'

Many grieving people have felt, with Jesus, 'My God, my God, why hast thou forsaken me?' or the complaint, 'God, how could you let an innocent child die?' Others think, 'What have I done to be punished so hard by fate?' Sometimes one sees with time that this process can give the grieving person a better-defined attitude to their faith, to the meaning of existence and to their own death.

Working on anger

Many people are afraid of anger. They believe that love and anger are mutually exclusive. It can be a great help to people to explain to them that anger and love belong together. In Bowlby's example, the young child kicks his mother. Minutes later he will be cuddling up on her lap! The anger is necessary in setting boundaries to others, and is thus part of work on the optimum distance. Clients who realize that by being angry they are not letting the dead person down become less afraid of expressing their anger.

There are great individual differences as to how intensely the anger is felt and against whom it is directed. For instance, Sandra felt anger against all women who were older than her mother. 'Why should they go on living when my mother was not allowed to?'

Work on anger is part of grief work whoever may be the object of the anger. There is energy and drive behind outward-directed anger. Used in the right way it can counteract the grieving person's apathy and increase their dynamism. So we should have no qualms about asking the mourner to visit or write to doctors, hospitals and so on to express their dissatisfaction, which does often contain an element of truth from which hospitals can learn.

We can ask the mourner to write about his anger with the deceased, with God, with all middle-aged women, possibly in letter form. We can also help the client to express the anger verbally either to the deceased's photograph or while visualizing the dead person in front of him. It may be done silently inside himself, or out loud so the therapist can follow it. When the anger is intense, it may be a relief to give physical expression to it: for instance, by thumping a pile of cushions and shouting the anger out. This can give a pleasant feeling of tiredness and relaxation of tension afterwards.

In their grief work some aggression-inhibited people experience an anger which they have never known before. In the longer term this gives them a chance to learn to say 'no' and thus achieve a more varied relationship to other people (the third task). But it is expedient to warn the bereaved person that initially his new behaviour can get him into some scrapes. When someone suddenly starts ticking off his friends for not understanding his grief, or telling his boss his unvarnished opinion of him, it does stir things up! Such experiences are part of the process someone has to go through if in a new phase of his life he is going to learn to handle anger. Some support from the therapist may be appropriate so that the anger does not become self-destructive.

Unfinished anger

> One of our clients was the widow of a house-painter whose brain was damaged by solvents. They had had many good years together before he fell ill. In the last six years of his life he was tyrannical and terrorized his family with his unpredictable fits of anger, which were due to his brain damage. Everyone in the family suffered from his unreasonable demands, but she could not be angry with him because his behaviour was caused by illness. The widow's grief work was lengthy and painful. For a long time she denied that she was angry with him. Not until after six months of intense pain and sense of loss could she admit to her anger at six years of ruined family life.

During the grief therapy she managed to write angry letters to her husband and by hard physical work in the garden she obtained some relief. She could then start on the final farewell, the fourth task. She is a good example of the fact that the anger one may feel against a tyrannical father or mother, a husband who beat you, a wife who deceived you, often does not come to the surface until after the person is dead.

If the grieving person is asked directly if he is angry with the deceased, he usually says 'no'. It is not the done thing to speak ill of the dead. If one wants to penetrate into the anger, it is wise first to ask in detail about what the grieving person misses. Then one can ask the question, '*And what don't you miss?*' a few times.

We have seen examples of unfinished anger being the only emotion a client had towards the deceased. However well-founded such anger may be, it will in time come to act as a defence against the positive feelings (however few these may be) which there always are in a close bond. Anger keeps the pain and the sense of loss at bay.

In other cases the complete absence of anger may be a problem. The personal account of a course of grief therapy which forms Chapter Six shows that there came an important turning-point in the process when, with some authority, the therapist confronted the client with her suppressed anger at her husband's suicide.

Bitterness

In the work of grief therapy, one regularly comes in contact with grieving people who are growing bitter at their fate. They often retreat into isolation because they think that nobody can really understand how difficult things are for them. The consequence may be that they develop chronic grief.

As a rule we ask clients straight out whether they are becoming bitter. We frequently get an affirmative answer. Many of them would like to be rid of the bitterness. We then explain that bitterness is a mixture of sadness and of anger. Only by separating out these two emotions will they be able, in the longer term, to get rid of the bitterness and sense of injustice. Again we use the technique of writing. The grieving person is asked to write a letter to us about his longings and sense of loss after the dead person, another letter about his anger. Gradually, as the clients can both sob with grief and express their anger, the bitterness diminishes.

Guilt

A certain feeling of guilt is a natural part of grief work. The grieving person wishes that she had not been snappy to her husband the day he had an accident. Or the widower wishes he had sent his wife to the doctor earlier. Some people feel that they ought to be grieving more – or differently. As a rule, these guilt feelings diminish by themselves with time. One can help the grieving person by asking him to describe all that he actually did. Sometimes this places the guilt feelings so much into perspective that they fade.

People who have a lot of anger in connection with the death often turn part of the anger inwards in the form of severe guilt feelings that can be difficult to work on directly. In Sandra's case we regarded the guilt feelings as a defence against the sense of loss and therefore chose to begin on them. When the guilt feelings also have an element of 'clinging' to the deceased, they can be hard to give up.

Shame

The psychoanalyst Erich Fromm thinks that loneliness is the main cause of the feeling of shame. When Adam and Eve were ashamed of their nakedness after eating the apple, it was not because they were shy about their genitals being visible, but because 'after man and woman have been separated and thus become aware of each other, they have realized the distance and difference between them, belonging as they do to two different sexes'. At the same time 'they also experience each other as strangers, because they have not yet learnt to love each other. Consciousness of human loneliness without union through love is the source of shame' (*The Art of Loving*, p. 25).

This description of shame harmonizes well with the observations we have made of shame in widows, widowers and parents whose children have died. Of course part of the shame is bound up with the reduced status which particularly widows have. They often have to move into a more modest home, their financial situation is reduced, and they are less in demand socially. However, the shame occurs too in women and men whose outward status has not been significantly lowered by the death. It is therefore probable that shame is bound up with the feeling of existential loneliness triggered off by the bereavement – loneliness which is so deep that one feels incapable of loving anyone any more. One is thus cut off from the fellowship of love.

Perhaps it is here too that we have to seek for the explanation of why it is so therapeutic for grieving people to share their feelings with others. The loving understanding which a mourner receives from others heals a little of the shameful loneliness. The grieving person is filled by the care and in it recovers *a little* of the feeling of being able to be fond of other people again.

Other component methods of grief therapy include the use of the following.

Pictures, objects and music

Photographs of the deceased may be useful in work on the second task. The people who find it hard to grieve often have difficulties in relating to pictures of the person they were fond of. For instance, Sandra had hidden away all the pictures of her mother. It became part of her grief work to bring them out and show the group those of them she liked most. Thus she had a picture of her mother in front of her in the group when she read aloud her letter to her mother.

Objects which have belonged to the dead person may have great symbolic significance. Sandra had inherited a bracelet from her mother, and she had hidden this away too, like the photos. As part of her work, we asked her to bring out the bracelet and find a constructive symbolic significance in it. Sandra decided that the bracelet was going to remind her of all the love and support she had got from her mother. Nobody could take away from her what was based on her childhood. In other words, the bracelet became a symbol of what she was *not* going to say goodbye to. The prospect of the final farewell (the fourth task) then became that little bit less daunting.

So if we therapists use our imagination, we can find many symbols and rituals which ease the client's work of grieving. Some people find great pleasure in music that calls forth strong and good memories. So music can also become part of grief work.

Letter-writing

The great majority of people find that writing letters to the person they have lost is a strong and meaningful experience. It is a method that makes it possible to bring out and deal with the emotions of grief in a particularly creative way. Sandra's letter to her mother came to signify an integration of the difficult emotions she had been through when she was working on her mother's death-bed. The letter, which was a home-work assignment, helped her to get into perspective the course of events that had been so frightening to her. When she read the letter aloud in the group, she once more came in contact with those deep emotions and was thus given a fresh opportunity of living through them, this time with less chaos.

Letter-writing can be used in many contexts. A grieving person may have got stuck in a tangle of feelings of guilt, loss and anger. Letters can be a great help in separating out the feelings. If someone writes a letter one day about the sense of loss, another a week later about guilt feelings, and then a third letter about their anger at being deserted, it makes for clarity and order. It reduces their fear and benefits their self-esteem. Sometimes the bereaved may need to tell her dead mother how life is going on without her, how the children are faring, and so on. In other cases there is a particular event that has to be raked over in one or several letters. A man who, after his wife's death, discovered that she had been unfaithful to him for a considerable time, needed to write a number of letters to her to clarify his feelings. All these letters are a good preparation for the final farewell. The final farewell letter is linked to the fourth task and should usually not be begun until six to twelve months after the death.

In the course of a bereavement, it may also be helpful to write to others than just the dead person. One may write to oneself to get various problem areas sorted out. One may write merely to give vent to one's feelings.

A 25-year-old widow was very angry with her mother-in-law, by whom she felt unfairly treated in connection with her husband's estate. This anger came to overshadow the loss of the husband. All attempts at talking to the mother-in-law were failures. After writing a furious letter to her mother-in-law in her diary, the widow had found an outlet for her anger and could then make progress in her grief work.

When suggesting to clients that they write letters as home assignments, we prepare them for the possibility that the writing may trigger off many difficult emotions. We therefore make sure that they will make use of their network if this is felt necessary. A woman who was working on her sister's suicide discovered by letter-writing how angry she was that her sister had chosen that way out. She had not previously felt anger with her sister and so was scared when in rage she cut her sister's picture into tiny pieces. She remembered our arrangement and contacted a woman friend with whom she had a good conversation.

It has been surprising to discover that practically *everyone* can write strong moving letters regardless of their schooling. So we can recommend anyone who has to go through grief work to write to the person they have lost. We have seen so many people benefit from this process that letter-writing ought to develop into a matter of course. It is a help in getting one's thoughts and feelings formulated and thus settling accounts with the past, to say 'thank you' for what one has received and 'goodbye' to what one has lost. In our society, we have so few rituals left. Letter-writing could become a new ritual that could support the natural work of grieving in a meaningful way.

The third task: the acquisition of new skills

The first two tasks of grief work are to accept that the loss is final and to deal with the feelings that arise from this acceptance. The third great task is to acquire new skills in contacts with other people and in accomplishing practical tasks.

There is a constant interplay in the work of the second and third tasks. Often the mourner will give way to her feelings while, perhaps for the first time in her life, she has to arrange a funeral and think of rituals. She thus has to attend to her feelings and simultaneously handle an unaccustomed task. These double demands, in which someone has to accommodate strong emotions and at the same time act on an external level, continue throughout the grief work. The problem presents itself in a clear-cut way when the person who has been lost was a spouse, and particularly when the spouses had a clear division of roles. If it was the woman who cooked and the man who hammered in the nails, then the one left behind has to learn to do what the other used to do. It is the same if it was the woman who kept up with friends and relatives and the man who negotiated with the Inland Revenue.

If someone succeeds in the third task, there are good chances of personal growth. If a person can establish a closer relationship with other people and meet new challenges, he or she gains in self-confidence and fulfilment. If someone withdraws into himself or gives up in the face of practical demands, he will feel life to be both poorer and more anxiety-ridden.

Using one's network in a new way

When clients are becoming able to enter into the emotions of grief, we explain to them how necessary it is to share their feelings with others. If we are doing group work, they experience on the spot what a relief it is to share their grief with others. If we are working with an individual client, he senses how pleasant it is that we are there to absorb the emotions. It is always our aim to get the clients to express their feelings to one or more of their own network as soon as possible. In this we encounter barriers of two kinds. One is that the clients flinch from the encroachment involved in allowing a family member or a friend to see their despair. The other is that many people are frightened by someone else's tears. They begin consoling the mourner, 'I'm sure everything will turn out all right' and so on. Usually this is because they feel powerless in the face of the mourner and do not know how to help when they feel that comfort is not possible. Unable to cope with this power-lessness, they resort to soothing platitudes, thus hampering the natural reaction of grief.

In practice these two barriers mean that great demands are made upon the grieving person. First, they have to overcome their own reluctance to show 'weakness', and then they have to explain to those around them that they feel a need to talk and weep, and perhaps rage. Mourners have to teach their friends just to listen without *doing* anything. It may feel very hard in the midst of our grief to have to 'educate' our network of friends. But if the work of grief is going to be finished, there is no escaping this. On a longer term we know that this opening-up on the part of the mourner can turn into the start of a contact with other people that has quite a new depth and intensity.

Part of our contact with the clients is almost always to give them tasks in using their network in a new way. A common dialogue in connection with such a task might be as follows:

'Who do you feel most secure with in your circle of friends?'
'Lucy.'
'Do you think Lucy would be able to bear seeing you cry, if you talk to her about how much you are missing Jane?'
'I don't really know.'
'Would you be able to explain to Lucy that she is not to comfort you but just listen and ask questions. To tell her that it would be a

help to you if she would listen and let you cry and perhaps put an
arm round you, but that she is not to comfort you?'
    'Yes, I think I could.'
    'Would you be willing to contact Lucy before the next session'
    'Yes, but it will be hard.'

It may sometimes be necessary for the therapists themselves to
contact the network if the client finds the idea too daunting. Just once we
contacted a workplace which our client found almost unendurable. The
client had lost a child, and her workmates were so upset for her that they
simply did not know what to do. There was silence when she appeared,
particularly if they were talking about children. She felt so isolated that
she was considering handing in her notice. So with the client's permis-
sion we contacted one of her most influential workmates and explained
to her that from time to time Irene needed to be able to talk about her
grief and maybe even to cry. It would be a help if they would enquire
how she was feeling and generally listen and be supportive. She did *not*
need to be over-protected by their keeping quiet about joys and sorrows
with their own children. If she did happen to cry, there must be room for
that. Her colleague quickly realized what we meant and was relieved at
being briefed like this. She had a word with the other employees about
changing their attitude to Irene.

We have had many encouraging examples of people being able and
willing to be supportive if only they are given a little help. Irene now felt
that she had the freedom to go in and out of her grief and in a natural way
to ask the others to listen. Many of them felt free to weep with Irene
about her loss.

New skills after losing a spouse

Alan's wife Jane died unexpectedly after a brief illness. Jane was
the active and outgoing one of the two. Alan was the creative and
more introspective one. Jane had seen to keeping contact with
their joint friends, and she was the one who wrote to the Inland
Revenue and other public bodies. Alan had been the support
backing her up. He had got her interested in literature and music.

After Jane's death Alan was lonely and in deep despair. He had
good contact with his emotions but had never shared personal
problems with anyone but Jane. So he did not need help with the
first and second tasks. By being in the group he got the necessary
help with the third task. Here, for the first time, this inhibited man
shared his feelings with others. It was the start of his being able to
practise greater openness to other people in general. We could
now begin to set him tasks with sharing his grief with friends and

neighbours. Jane had always wished Alan to be more open towards other people, and it was hard for him to admit that this did not become possible until Jane was dead. Alan had to train himself in a new role when in company, and he had to learn to use his network as a partial replacement for Jane. It was a great grief to him that she was not able to join in this positive new development.

When snags occurred with the couple's building project, Alan had to take on the difficult battles with the local council and thus he also developed new skills in that area.

Overcoming fear after a trauma

It was a shock for Eileen one morning to find her husband dead beside her in bed. She became so afraid of sleeping in the flat that a year later she still did not dare to be at home alone. She and her baby stayed with her parents. Dependence on the parental milieu became more and more of a strain. In the group, with anxiety and weeping, she had been working on re-living the traumatic situation when she woke up and found Ivan dead (the second task). The next aim was to accomplish the third task: to dare to be alone in the flat with her baby. She was particularly afraid of seeing the bed again. We suggested that the first few times she should get a woman friend to sleep with her. We asked her to brief the friend to go with her to the bed while she told about the morning when she had found her husband dead. She was to go into details about what she had seen, heard, felt and done. In other words, she was now to re-live the whole situation along with her friend. The first nights, as arranged, she slept at the flat with her woman friend but without the baby. Then the baby also began to be there with them. Over a week or so she thus began the 'reconquest' of her home by living an everyday life there. After ten days the next task was for her to sleep there one night alone with the baby. We helped her as to how she was to deal with her anxiety when she was alone. Who could she phone if it got too much? We prepared her that she might not be able to sleep for the first few nights.

Eileen had to regain her territory. Not until then would she be able to decide whether she would stay on at the flat with the traumatic memories. After a fortnight Eileen decided that she would probably stay at the flat after all. She had vowed that she never would when she started in the grief group.

Personal growth

Eileen had now to begin on a new and more independent way of life. In many different ways she had to develop new skills and overcome anxiety. Her next task was to begin to feel she was 'Eileen' and not half of a couple called 'Eileen and Ivan'. For more than a year she had avoided social life in spite of many invitations. Although she found it hard to be alone, she was unable to be with other people on an informal level. After starting in the group she was able to talk about her loneliness after her husband's death, about her problems and to weep over her bereavement with her friends. On the other hand, if she was with people who were not aware of her grief, she became anxious. To such a degree was her identity bound up with her deceased husband that she felt incapable of functioning on her own. She was threatened with chronic grief, not because she did not dare to feel the necessary pain (the second task), but because she did not consider she was worth being with as a single person. Her grief also protected her against unpleasant new demands, and this would be her 'gain' from the grief becoming chronic.

Before she could leave the group, the aim was not only that she should be able to enter *into* her grief and feel what she had lost, but also that she should be able to come *out of* her grief and be in other people's company in an undemanding way. She trained herself in this by (for instance) being the listener at the coffee table after the group work.

If Eileen had not been given help in the third task, she would probably have escaped headlong into a new couple relationship, in order not to feel like half a couple among other people. So Eileen made good progress in her self-confidence training. Her husband's death came to mean the acquisition of skills which this dependent woman had never had before. The grief work ended up by giving her a new quality in company with other people. She was pleased about these new experiences, but at the same time had to battle with guilt feelings that Ivan had to die before she could acquire sufficient courage and insight to open up to other people. Eileen's example shows that the third task does not only mean that some quite necessary challenges are met in order to establish a reasonably normal life after a loss; it also opens ways to a more healthy and whole life.

The reactions of the network to changes

In Chinese 'crisis' and 'change' are the same word, a linguistic expression of the age-old recognition that there can be personal growth in crisis and grief. After a profound emotional shake-up in which we overcome anxiety and confusion in order to meet new challenges, we are no longer the same as we were. In Chapter One we have already described the more profound personality aspects of this change. Here we shall only mention the self-esteem which work on the third task may give to many people. They become better at differentiating between what is essential and what is inessential, and they become more courageous. They often become better at putting limits on themselves and at saying 'no'. But these changes may seem overwhelming not only to the mourner, who may be amazed at the strength he has within him, but also for his network, who are accustomed to seeing him in a particular role. When in connection with grief a reticent and inhibited person begins to ask for help and show emotions and perhaps even opt out of certain situations, the change may be overwhelming to his family and friends. We have had to prepare clients that those close to them will feel most secure if they remain as they always have been – and that they must give their acquaintances time to get used to the mourner's new way of being. In some cases we have, with the client, had to admit that some of those in the network were unable to tolerate the new behaviour, but that has been rare.

We have had a number of examples of people in support roles keeping the mourner in a dependent relationship longer than necessary. Parents of young people who, for instance, have lost a boyfriend or girlfriend, or have become seriously ill, may easily be tempted to feel that they have got their 'child' back.

Happily, the changed behaviour most often leads to positive changes in relationships with friends and family. Such a change is described by Jytte, who had been through grief therapy in connection with a physical handicap:

> I have acquired quite an incredible amount of ballast here. When I think back to a year ago when my colleague at work had an operation for breast cancer, then I crawled away and hid, excusing my lack of contact by saying that I was mentally unable to cope with it. Today, when the same colleague had another lump removed, I phoned her, though I realized beforehand that both she and I would cry. I have really learnt how important it is to talk openly about feelings, even if it isn't pleasant....

Summing up the third task

In the third task the grieving person has to learn to *act* in new ways. The therapist should therefore have his focus all the time on the new skills which the mourner needs in everyday life. As far as treatment is concerned this means that, with the client, we try to pinpoint the new challenges which the mourner will have to meet. It may be anything from cooking, daring to go to an over-sixties club, contacting people, overcoming fear of places associated with the death, going to social gatherings alone, learning to say 'no', learning to ask for help, learning to show emotions, and much besides.

It may be useful to make contracts with the client about which new challenges she will try to meet before the next meeting with the therapist. It goes without saying that it is important to find the right time for the right challenges. Mild pressure from the therapist may be necessary, because the client has to try something new and so has a natural nervousness. The client has to learn to put up with his heart thumping and his hands sweating, which always accompanies the exceeding of boundaries. But he needs much support and backing from the therapist. If the contract is not kept, the therapist has to weigh up whether the task was set at too early a stage or if it was too hard for the client. If, for instance, it proves too hard to go along to an over-sixties club alone, a new task might be to have a cup of tea with the woman next door and possibly get her to go along too the first few times. The therapist has to be inventive and flexible.

It is a golden rule to start with the easy tasks and make them harder as one goes along. It is not crucial for the outcome of a task to be the one the client had hoped for. A bad outcome may be an invaluable learning process. Example: many people feel that they will not be able to get over a refusal, if they open up to a friend and ask for help. It can be a useful experience for someone to sustain a refusal without completely losing his self-confidence. We are much better equipped for daring to contact others if we have learnt that we can stand a defeat. It is only from passivity that no one learns anything.

At one point we had a trainee who helped a client who had got stuck on the third task, by saying: 'Someone who ventures, loses his footing for a while. Someone who ventures nothing, loses himself.' The third task of grief work is to venture something new.

The fourth task: reinvesting emotional energy

The fourth task is to be able to achieve the final farewell so as to be ready to make other attachments again. It is to be able to reinvest one's emotional energy in new relationships and in new ways.

Sigmund Freud is clear in his description of the aim of grief work. He emphasizes that the function of grief is to detach from the deceased the thoughts and hopes of those left behind. So the mourner has to withdraw his psychological energy from the person or thing he has lost. We use the expression that a 'tombstone' has to be erected. One has to say goodbye in order later to be able to say hello.

When our spouse dies, we have to say goodbye to all our joint hopes, dreams and plans for the future. Our thoughts and feelings have slowly to let go of the dead one. The wound left by the death has to be healed so that we can become a whole person again with the dead person as a fond memory. We have to *say the final farewell.*

Some clients need it to be stressed that the final farewell is *not* a farewell to all memories of the departed. Time is an important factor. The second and third tasks have to be gone through many times before a person is ready for the final farewell.

The natural process cannot be speeded up, even by therapy. In cases of severe loss, it will be at least nine to twelve months before we are ready to approach the final farewell and begin to withdraw our energy from the deceased. It will normally be two to three years before we are really open to new relationships. It is usual to reckon that, for instance, a divorce takes at least two years.

A mother who had lost her 10-year-old daughter told us, 'Now I have nobody left I am fond of.' She had four other children! All her energy, even six months after the death, was bound up in the grief, so that she could not feel anything for others. Worden uses the expression 'to love again' as the measure of how far someone has come through the fourth task. In this context loving again means to be prepared to live through the grief which a new loss in one's life would entail. 'The cost of commitment is grief' is a famous quotation from Parkes's book on grief.

A woman was referred to us who, two years after the death of her youngest child, had had the three eldest children placed in care outside the home. She had been incapable of living through a farewell to the dead child, and on an unconscious level had safe-guarded herself against feeling pain in connection with the three eldest children by never committing her feelings to them again. She thus protected herself by ensuring that there were no more close attachments to lose.

Work on the fourth task

The emotional work on the first three tasks leads on to the final farewell. The first task is the recognition that the loss is a reality, the second task is feeling the pain and the third task is the acquisition of new skills to make a new life possible. We have previously mentioned how poor our culture is in rituals able to support the work of grief. In the old days people put away a black arm-band or black clothes after a certain length of time. This symbolized the transition to a new life without the dead person.

The farewell letter to the deceased is a new and good ritual. It is often prepared for by a series of other letters, as mentioned under the second task. In the last letter, stock is taken of the relationship, and the letter is finished off with 'goodbye', often an immensely hard word to write and say aloud. The reading aloud of this letter to the dead person is a ritual marking the transition to a new phase of the person's life. The dead person will no longer be in command. Energy wells up for other activities and for reaching out to other people again. The dead person will not be forgotten, but the memory will be like a bitter-sweet pain. The tears will change from ones of despair to ones of sadness. The goal is for the memories of the dead child, the dead partner, to be given their place in everyday life in a natural way.

One of our clients who had spent much energy on her grief work over a long period came back to the grief group one day and with much energy informed them that *now* her late husband would have to look after himself. In a symbolic way this decision gives an excellent feeling of what the fourth task contains.

When the final farewell is omitted

There are many people who live a long life without ever quite letting go of the divorced partner or of their dead ones. They are rarely bothered by symptoms other than some anxiety linked to other people. But if they sustain fresh losses, the old unfinished grief may be opened up again. Then there is again a chance that the old grief work can be finished off with a final farewell. If this does not happen, the grief at the new loss can only be resolved at the same level as the grief at the old loss. This means that the mourner's functional level declines after the new loss, because there are now two unfinished losses. So each fresh loss can be regarded as a turning-point.

> An example of the consequences of becoming afraid of committing oneself emotionally again after a loss is Kirsten, who was referred to us three months after her husband Sam suddenly died from a blood clot. She had thoughts of suicide and experienced intense anxiety. It turned out that her first husband, Peter, had died six years before after twenty-five years of marriage. That time she had 'coped wonderfully', had looked after her children and begun her work in a senior post a few weeks after the death. But ever since her first husband's death, Kirsten had been afraid of attaching herself to anyone again. She had had a lot of anxiety in her, which she had partially suppressed by will power and in the first period with tranquillizers.
> Gradually she had settled down fairly well on her own. She had

been hard to persuade to move in with her new husband. But she had done so and had had a happy time, even though her fear of losing him loomed in the background. Then after a year and a half of marriage he suddenly died.

Kirsten had not severed her ties to her first husband. The grief work over her second husband had therefore to include her grief over her first. The acute grief at Sam's death quickly paved the way for weeping over the loss of Peter. In the first weeks the 'double' grief and pain were indescribably great. Her grown-up children and family had to support her through these difficult weeks when she was on sick leave. It was quite a new experience for her to give way and accept help. After this, the way was prepared for her farewell letter to Peter. Later there followed long and painful grief work over Sam, into which naturally the grief over Peter constantly intertwined. The grief work with Sam took up so much more time because it was more recent and because it entailed a farewell to the whole life to which she had so hesitantly said 'yes': a home, prestige, a secure financial situation – a joint everyday life and the dream of growing old together.

With the help of friends she was able to manage this grief work herself, after breaking the ties to her first husband and thus overcoming her fear of her pain. If Kirsten had not been given help, her future would have been endangered. A normal network cannot absorb the pain of bidding farewell to two spouses at one time.

Guilt and shame at investing in a new life

Many people who have lost a child or a marriage partner find that choosing to lead a life without pain but with joy and growth brings emotions of guilt and shame. The feeling of letting down the dead may therefore be an obstacle to investing their energy in a new life.

One of our clients with an avoided grief reaction of ten years' standing wrote in her farewell letter to her baby:

When they came with the little coffin I was almost turned to stone, I only shed a single tear. The sky above us was azure, and deep down inside I was praying for autumn, winter and cold. For ten years I have lived with it. Little Carol, at that time I felt that, *since you did not exist any more, how could I allow myself feelings like joy, grief and contact*. Not until today, so many years later, can I say 'Goodbye, little Carol.' The grief which then should have arisen as a natural result of losing the dearest thing I had possessed, I have passed through now. I have wept, suffered and mourned, so that my heart was breaking. Carol, it helped; I am living with your memory as something dear, and I am glad that today I can say goodbye to you, something I never managed to do. Therefore I can now live and again let the sun shine.

It is important to be aware of this feeling of guilt right from an early point in every grief work. It is paralysing for someone to feel that they are letting down the person they have lost if they enjoy themselves and forget their grief. The guilt feelings may grow even greater if those around expect a certain behaviour if the mourner is not to be regarded as shallow. When the guilt feelings bind someone's energy to the dead person, it can inhibit an otherwise healthy grieving process.

A woman who lost both her children in dramatic circumstances underwent a healthy and natural grieving process in the year or so that she was attached to the group. Her grief work succeeded in giving her a growing strength and deeper relationships with other people. This good development, however, was often hampered by guilt feelings at allowing herself to feel any joy after losing her children. She worked on this guilt feeling in the group. We supported her in the idea that she had honestly earned her progress by the courageous and difficult grief work she had passed through.

Again and again we see people gaining a new and often stronger and more intense life despite recurring pain at their loss. Another woman wrote in her farewell letter to the group:

> To me, and I know to several in the group, it seems a cruel and bitter irony that the broad view, the insight cannot be known until everything is too late. Irrevocably too late, if it's to be with those we have loved who now are dead. But the pain at this very thing conceals the challenge that it is not too late with those who are left behind. There is a strength of life to be lived. Something good and something bad will happen to all of us here, but we have the potential to relate to our destiny in a different way from before.

That is the essence of the fourth task.

Chapter three

Risk groups and factors in deciding treatment

One of the most famous pathological grief reactions in world literature is seen in Ophelia in Shakespeare's *Hamlet*. Ophelia goes mad and ends by drowning herself because her betrothed, Hamlet, has killed her beloved father. If Ophelia had been given help to accommodate her many warring emotions, her insanity and suicide might have been avoided. Ophelia and Hamlet might have lived happily ever after, but humanity would have been deprived of a mighty tragedy.

When a therapist is faced with an 'Ophelia' who has suffered a great loss, there are three parameters which it may be useful to apply in order to identify whether she should be given preventive help for her grief work. We use the term 'parameters', because it is the interrelation of the three factors that determines the assessment.

The three parameters are:

1 the circumstances around the loss;
2 the mourner's personality and attachment to the person or thing she has lost;
3 the mourner's psycho-social circumstances.

The circumstances around the loss

Was it a sudden and 'untimely' death? A divorce without warning? A completely unexpected diagnosis? Was it an event which at one stroke changed the mourner's situation in life, or had there been time for an adjustment process? Was it a peaceful death, an accident, a traumatic course of illness, a suicide or a murder? Had the spouses parted more or less amicably, or had the divorce been tough, humiliating and hurtful?

The question can be phrased like this: How great a trauma has the mourner undergone? A trauma may be so shattering to the soul that it can block normal grief work.

The mourner's personality and attachment to the person or thing she has lost

This is the most difficult parameter to assess, because there are so many different factors present here. A thorough analysis of what the mourner, with her particular personality, has been deprived of by the loss in question gives the best understanding of the grief.

The grief work is shaped by the relationship to the deceased. Was the attachment healthy and natural, or was the relationship symbiotic or ambivalent?

The grief differs depending upon the stage of life of the person. If a woman loses a breast, the grief is greater if she is young than if she is an older woman to whom physical appearance counts less. The main rule is that the more harmonious the relationship is to the person or thing lost, the less prone the mourner will be to a pathological course of grief. The grief work is made harder the more complicated the various 'losses within the loss' are for the mourner.

The mourner's psycho-social circumstances

This parameter particularly concerns the mourner's network. Is there someone who can accommodate the mourner's emotions? Is there anyone who can provide practical support? Is there adequate cultural and religious support for (as an example) immigrants? The answers that the therapist receives to these questions will have great influence upon whether professional help should be provided in the first period after the loss.

We also have to assess whether the mourner has practical and financial possibilities for obtaining peace and quiet for her energy-demanding grief work.

In England Parkes has done pioneering work in pinpointing those mourners who are particularly at risk. This chapter is based on his findings.

In the rest of this chapter we have chosen deaths as the losses at the centre of the grief work. Of course the parameters may be applied analogously to other kinds of loss.

The first parameter: the circumstances around the loss

How did the death occur?

A death may occur in many ways. Some people die peacefully in their sleep, others may have an accident and die in great pain.

The timing of the death may be more or less appropriate in the course of a person's life. It may be a natural conclusion to a long life, or it may strike a child, a young person or someone in the prime of life.

The way the death occurred and the age of the victim have proved to have great influence upon the grief reactions of the bereaved. All things being equal, it is easier to process a loss for which there has been good time to prepare, in which death occurs relatively peacefully and in which the deceased was elderly.

If death comes about in a sudden and dramatic manner, the person left behind may sustain a shock that can block the healthy grief process if it is not worked upon. A person's mind is shaken up by having to face without warning news that a son has been killed in a road accident, that a spouse has fallen down dead with a heart attack, or that someone close to them has committed suicide or been murdered. The world may suddenly appear to them as a hostile and unpredictable environment. The dominant emotions will be helplessness and fear. In a violent way they are confronted with the fact that the influence and control they have over their own lives is limited. In order not to be completely swamped by hopelessness and impotence, the psyche will react with various useful mechanisms. A sense of unreality, guilt, anger, vengefulness are common reactions just after a death. All these emotions serve the healthy purpose of limiting the feeling of helplessness and of protecting against the overwhelming fear. In literature this phase is described as the normal state of crisis, in which after the shock we realize and accept what has happened stage by stage, so that the mind can keep in step. In this section on *traumatic deaths*, we have chosen to review actual assessments in relation to *accident cases, acute illness, suicide, murder and two deaths closely following each other in the immediate family*.

The overall theme will be why these particular clients are in the risk group measured by the three parameters.

Accidental death

A 20-year-old woman was referred to us six months after the death of her fiancé in an accident at work. She spent a month by his sick-bed while he hovered between life and death. Her experiences in connection with the death had been so stressful that six months afterwards she was still living in a state of unreality. She felt empty, dreary and indifferent about everything and everyone, and emotionally she had not admitted that the fiancé was dead. All her thoughts still focused on the stay in hospital when she had been strong and supportive throughout. Her fiancé had been her best friend since she was 16. They had both moved from the provinces, and her network was thin on the ground.

The first parameter was seriously affected, because the circumstances were very stressful. The second parameter was more slightly affected, because this was a very close but otherwise apparently normal attachment. The third parameter was perhaps the determining one. In the very difficult period at the hospital she had been emotionally isolated, because her friends and family lived in the provinces. Only very few people can work through alone the kind of strain she had been under before her friend died.

A woman of 45 was still emotionally blocked eight months after her grown-up daughter had been killed in a road accident. She did not weep, but spent all her energy on the events of the day of the accident and her violent anger against the motorist. The trauma of the death stood between her and normal grief work. She had lost her child, but it was the anger that filled her. She could not use an otherwise well-functioning network, because she did not want to get started on the necessary pain of having to say farewell to her daughter.

The first parameter was seriously affected by the sudden death in a road accident. The second parameter was probably the determining one, as she proved to have had a very close, almost symbiotic relationship to her daughter. The third parameter appeared normal. There was time, tranquillity and emotional space around her for her grief work. But she was unable to make use of her network because of the circumstances around the death and her attachment to her daughter.

In these two cases pathological grief was developing. There was a need for grief therapy to break the emotional block so that the two women could start the four tasks of grief work.

Death after acute illness

A typical example of a reaction to an unexpected death is 30-year-old Sandy. A month and a half before his referral to us, his wife had died under an anaesthetic. She was going to have a minor routine operation, but under the anaesthetic the doctors discovered a life-threatening disease, and she bled to death during the operation. For the first few days after her death, Sandy had been numbed, just staring blankly and feeling that it couldn't have happened to him. He had slowly emerged from this state of unreality and was able to enter into despair and hopelessness and cry a lot. But for many months he went on seeing his wife sitting in her usual chair in front of the television. When he came home and saw his wife's jacket hanging in the hall, he always found himself thinking: 'Oh good, she's come home', before reality caught up with him. For periods he was afraid of going mad. Her nightdress in the bed still smelled slightly of her, and every night he fell asleep with it under his cheek.

Sandy was a man of rather inhibited aggression, so he found it frightening that he felt *violent anger* against the hospital where she died. He felt that the doctors must have made a mistake – she had been quite fit when she went in. He also had a great *need to understand* the course of the operation and the serious disease. A long and thorough interview with the consultant surgeon made it plain to him that the doctors had done their utmost to save his wife, and that she would have died within a short time and in great pain if she had not been operated upon. Although Sandy accepted this explanation, his violent anger did not go away. He was also very *angry with his network*, which he felt was not giving him the necessary support. As he was not religious and so could not be angry with God or fate, he directed all his anger against the doctors and his network.

He also had a *need to recount the whole course of events* right from the first symptom which led to his wife going into hospital. His conversations with the doctor before the operation, his last contact with his wife, the ordeal of laying her in her coffin, and the subsequent conversations with the doctors had to be gone over again and again. This whole course of events had been so traumatic that he had a strong urge to talk and weep his way out of it. In his thoughts he reviewed the time before the hospitalization and had some *guilt feelings* that he had not got his wife to the doctor earlier, although this would probably not have altered the outcome very much.

Sandy's grief work a month and a half after this traumatic death was quite natural. The reason that we agreed to give him professional grief help was the following assessment. Sandy felt that from one day to the next he had lost part of himself. He had been almost *symbiotically attached to his wife* since he was 19, when she became the centre of his life. They had had no children. She had been the one who provided for emotional contact with their circle of friends, so he was without any training in using other people as a network.

This overlapping of various circumstances in which all three parameters were 'showing yellow and red' made us think that it was right to offer him preventive help – for instance, by supporting him in using the network he did in fact have. Sandy's risk was a chronic development of grief.

An example where the circumstances surrounding a death may be so frightening that it was not enough either that there was a good network or that the attachment to the deceased was unremarkable, is Ellen, aged 70. Four months after the death she was still troubled by the sight she saw when her husband died in convulsions. She was alone with him when he died. She reproached herself for not having learnt cardiac massage. She had nightmares every night.

The first parameter was so strongly affected that the very traumatic experience was in itself causing a pathological state. The second and third parameters could not be assessed in this case as long as the trauma obscured the grief work. In order to process the trauma, Ellen needed help in the form of crisis intervention.

Suicide

The suicide of a close relative is one of the most difficult losses to get over. The mourner is left with a welter of contradictory emotions: anger, shame, guilt and bereavement. At the same time the mourner often has a feeling of having been rudely cast off by the deceased. The situation is, of course, particularly complicated if the bereaved had a conflict with the dead person when he took his own life.

So the grieving person faces the complex task of unravelling the many emotions. A young woman whose father committed suicide wrote the following:

A week before his death we had talked about going to the USA together. Deep down I knew that it was a dream which I so intensely hoped would become reality. It was too late. My aunt phoned to say they had found him dead. He had hanged himself. It put an end to my faith in other people and myself. I had not measured up. I began to believe it was my fault that my father had committed suicide. I have been feeling that for the last five years.

The bereaved family often help to produce *distorted communication* by talking about the suicide in euphemisms as a tragic accident. In some families the cause of death becomes a secret which sets a distance to those family and friends who do not know it. In that way the secret contributes to the grievers' isolation.

The shame, the feeling of guilt and identification with the dead may often bring about thoughts of suicide in the bereaved or some other self-destructive behaviour like isolation, alcohol- or drug-abuse. Some clients will openly say that they feel a need to be punished because they feel they have so signally failed.

An example of grief reaction after a suicide is 23-year-old Lizette, whose mother committed suicide shortly after quarrelling with her. Lizette was an only child and had been alone with her mother for many years. The mother had had rather a miserable life and had always leaned on her daughter with a need for sympathy and care. All through Lizette's childhood her mother had frequently threatened suicide. Lizette had done her best to humour her mother. A few days before her mother's suicide, Lizette, backed up by her fiancé, had finally spoken out against her mother's endless complaints and had made known to her that she would now have to manage on her own. Lizette had her own life to run. The mother again threatened suicide, and Lizette answered angrily that if she wanted to commit suicide then she could. Lizette wasn't going to keep her alive any more. A few days later the mother hanged herself.

Lizette applied for help six months after her mother's death. She was troubled by violent guilt feelings and almost constantly felt aware of her mother's reproachful presence in her flat. She particularly sensed her accusing glances upon her. She was ashamed at her mother's suicide, which she felt as a great personal defeat, and so she had not told her friends about it. When they talked about their own parents, she kept quiet. This had gradually created a distance to her circle of friends and made her very isolated. Her fiancé had often repeated that it was not her fault that her mother killed herself, but that had not eased her guilt feelings. On the contrary, her *self-confidence*, which was *low* anyway, had become lower than ever. She felt that by her death her mother had *rejected* her and her love more effectively than she could have done in any other way. For a period she had thoughts of suicide and *punished* herself by isolating herself from her friends, who frequently tried to hold on to her. When she was due to take an exam, she withdrew, because she felt that she had not deserved to pass.

Under the surface anger was constantly smouldering, which at first she used self-destructively. She was not particularly aware of how angry she was, but when in her despair she shouted 'Why did you do it?', it was not hard to hear the underlying anger. 'Why did you do this *against me*?' This understandable anger often lies hidden under the many different feelings that arise in connection with suicide.

If we look at the parameters, then the first parameter is nearly always affected in a dramatic way when suicide is the cause of death. In Lizette's case she was exposed to a shock, and naturally enough was in crisis for about a week. If she had herself found her mother dead, the first parameter would have been even more affected. For then the crisis would also have been affected by the visual impression which we have described in the example of Ellen.

The second parameter was the determining factor, because Lizette's attachment to her mother was unusually ambivalent. The third parameter was not particularly affected. Lizette had a fiancé who could more or less accommodate her emotions. She had a network which could provide her with care. Being a student, she was in a practical position to have both time and tranquillity for her grief work.

Despite her good outward conditions, Lizette needed professional help. Her 'wound in the soul' was so complicated that if it were to have a chance to heal, grief therapy was a necessity.

Another example from our work is Connie, aged 48, whose 24-year-old son committed suicide after failing a final examination. Connie had apparently been relatively well functioning as a mother, a wife and at her workplace until her son's death. After the son's suicide she became more and more self-destructive. She began to drink, gave notice at work, stayed in bed for days, and isolated herself in her shame. Apparently she had a need both to punish herself and to identify with her son, who had been very self-destructive in the period before the suicide.

A year after her loss she was admitted to a psychiatric ward and thus was given an adequate sense that society was also punishing her. However, her guilt feelings did not abate.

Two years later she was referred to us, without our being able to help her in the chronic condition in which by then she was. Connie's future looked as if it would be an existence of unemployment, alcohol abuse and periodic admissions to psychiatric hospitals. If she had been given therapeutic help and not just tranquillizers in the months after her son's suicide, it is possible that this course of events might have been avoided.

In our grief group we have particularly encountered three categories of bereaved people who are at risk of pathological grief after a suicide. These are: young people whose parents have committed suicide; parents whose grown-up children have committed suicide; people whose spouses have committed suicide. If we look at the parameters, both the first and second groups have been affected in such a way that the bereaved will practically always be in the risk group. There are of course individual differences as to the healthiness of the attachment. All the same, we have gradually come to the conclusion that these three categories of bereaved ought to be offered grief help or grief therapy in order to prevent a pathological development.

Murder

Murder, like suicide, brings a sudden loss for which someone is normally quite unprepared. If the mourner has also been present at the murder, there are also both the *shocking experience and the feeling of guilt* at not having been able to prevent it. If the murder occurs within the family, there is the complicating factor that the mourner often both hates and at the same time is attached to the murderer. It can be very hard to accommodate this *ambivalence*. A woman whose husband killed their two children in a fit of jealousy had not only lost her children, but also her husband and companion of fifteen years. It was a great relief for her that we both understood and supported her grief at the loss of the husband, grief which her network was unable to accommodate. Her anger at him did not come till much later.

Most murders probably occur within the family. So the first two parameters are affected in just as complicated a way as we have described for suicide. This means that even under the best imaginable circumstances the network of the bereaved will hardly be a sufficient help in ensuring that the grief work develops naturally. In other words, we do not think that the *third* parameter has any major role in the assessment of whether the bereaved are in the risk group. Murder within the family will under all circumstances be so traumatic that crisis or grief help ought to be provided immediately after the murder has taken place. On a longer term it must be weighed up whether grief therapy will be necessary.

Several losses at once

Experience shows that if a person suffers a number of serious losses within a short time, the process always becomes complicated. Each loss requires its grief work. Two concurrent losses trigger off two different kinds of grief work, and the mind finds it hard to contain them at one time. If someone loses both his children in the same accident, it is therefore natural for his feelings to concern themselves particularly with one in one period and with the other in another period. Without help this can become unnecessarily complicated, because the grieving mother or father has guilt feelings towards the child with which they are *not* concerned at the time in question.

An example of a mourner with two losses is 60-year-old Elsie, who within a month lost both her husband and her adult daughter. In some periods the grief over her husband dominated, at others grief over her daughter. She was fond of them both in different ways, so the pain of the losses was different. Her grief work required so many resources that she was off sick for a considerable time. It cost extra strength to separate out the two grief reactions.

When, like Elsie, someone is afflicted by two losses at once, they are almost always in the risk group.

Getting two or more processes of grief work separated out in a useful way is a complicated task. It normally requires professional intervention. In relation to the separate losses, we can use the parameters in our assessment. In Elsie's case, both deaths occurred suddenly and in a traumatic way. In connection with the second and third parameters, there were no noteworthy features. Her attachment to both her husband and daughter had been normal and her network was good. All the same, she needed professional grief help, because the losses together exerted such great pressure that the normal grief work would have been too stressful without the help of the grief group.

The second parameter: the mourner's personality and attachment to the person or thing she has lost

The grieving person's personality and attachment to the deceased is the most difficult of the parameters to assess. The rule of thumb is that the more clear-cut and emotionally satisfying a relationship is, the healthier is the course of the grief work. When we are to use this parameter, it is therefore a help to start out from the attachment in order to understand what the mourner is up against in having to bid farewell to the deceased.

It is useful to understand the difference between love and dependency. Bowlby stresses that when a relationship between two people contains love, then they can tolerate separation. For they have confidence that the other will return when necessary. If we use Bowlby's concept of 'optimum distance', that means that the relationship is flexible, because one can feel secure when there is both distance and proximity to the other person.

When there is more dependency than love in the relationship, there is not this flexibility. The partners will therefore in a rigid way seek to keep a certain distance from each other, so that the relationship becomes strained.

What characterizes healthy grief work is the ability to go in and out of the emotions of grief. The grieving person must, in other words, have the requisite flexibility to be able, even in his grief, to tolerate closeness to as well as distance from the deceased. In the rigid relationship this ability has not been developed, and so the grief reaction will develop pathologically. It will become either chronic or avoided grief.

In the following we shall review various types of attachments between people in order to clarify the second parameter. This time we shall omit the other parameters as part of the assessment. The relation between the parameters was surveyed in the last section.

Grief work when the attachment is normal

If we lose someone with whom we have had a good, lively emotional relationship, the pain is naturally very deep. We recall with sorrow all the good times when we enjoyed each other's company. We know that the relationship was mutual. It was a relationship in which problems were faced and solved, which means that the bereaved person does not have a lot of loose ends and unclarified feelings about the deceased. There is a great sense of loss, but complicating emotions like guilt and shame are only present to a natural and thus limited extent. There may be some anger that the deceased has deserted us, but that does not as a rule frighten the mourner.

A person who has had such a relationship with someone else will have developed a relatively good basic security, to use Erik Erikson's phrase. So as a rule he will also have a reasonably good network around him, and does not have to overcome much reluctance within himself to make use of it. The grieving person has experienced security and warmth in relationship to the deceased and will therefore have some confidence that others will be able to provide something similar. Self-esteem will be reasonably good, and that will make it possible for the mourner to accept support and care. Often the mourner will also have a good and secure feeling of the deceased's presence. This person will rarely be referred to professional help unless some of the other parameters tip the scale. He or she will cope with their grief work with the aid of the network.

A close but complicated attachment

As a general rule we may say that the more contradictory feelings someone has in relation to the deceased (consciously or unconsciously), and the less capable someone is of making contact with their emotions, then the greater is the risk of a pathological development of grief.

An imagined example of a person with many contradictory feelings might be a woman, Edna, whose husband Geoffrey has died of a long-lasting cancerous disease. In their twenty-five years of marriage she was very dependent on Geoffrey. She did not have outside work, she allowed him to decide everything, and she had his opinions. Edna was the typical 'self-sacrificing' wife. They never quarrelled, due to their joint understanding that they 'just had to make a go of things'. This widow of 50 has a tough job of grief work ahead. She is feeling deserted and her self-confidence is low.

Neither of them dared to mention that he was going to die, and so there are many things they did not manage to talk through. Her unconscious anger at having been kept down over many years makes it hard to her to feel his loss thoroughly. Perhaps too Edna has guilt feelings about something which she did not do well enough in connection with his illness and death. It will be even harder if she is also ashamed of becoming a widow at so young an age. The bereavement and the pain are also tinged with guilt, shame and repressed anger. She is now paying the price for her great dependence upon him. Edna's grief work is under threat. She risks either chronic grief or avoided grief, depending upon what she has learnt about expressing feelings in her childhood home.

It is our experience that people who have difficulties with the grief process because of contradictory emotions which they find hard to accommodate and so cannot express have had a childhood in which their attention was to a high degree directed towards satisfying their parents' emotional needs and suppressing their own genuine feelings, as we have described in Chapter One.

Edna doubtless grew up in a family which fits this description. But the suppression of emotions may have taken various forms. We must assume that it will be these subtle differences that determine the course of Edna's grief and the degree of risk she is at.

If Edna has learned that one ought not to show one's feelings, she will avoid entering into the emotions of grief. She will try to pull herself together, will generally withdraw from life, and will often become a frequent visitor to the doctor with physical and/or nervous symptoms.

If she also suffered a loss in childhood – for example, if she lost a parent – she will probably not have been given support in grieving. She will have learnt through this that a loss is not something to cry about. It must be reiterated here that we believe that if, after her husband's death, she is given help in processing his death, then her grief over the dead parent will probably emerge automatically. So at the same time she will be getting the chance to start on the old grief work. This will give her an opening to change the attitude she learned in childhood that feelings ought to be suppressed.

If she enters a state of chronic grief, we must presume that her experience in childhood was rather different. It was permissible to show 'upsetness', but not anger. She may also have received extra attention – that is, reward – when she was upset. In her chronic grief she will concentrate on the memory of her husband, just as she concentrated on his person while he lived. She will probably have frequent bouts of tearfulness, and even several years after his death she will find it hard to show interest in anything but her dead husband, and she will idealize their relationship.

This sketch of a loss with two possible courses of grief is of course highly schematized. What we have wanted to show is that strong dependency in relation to the deceased gives the risk of a pathological course of grief, and that ultimately the course of grief is determined by the childhood experiences which the mourner brings to it.

When the relationship is emotionally distant

If we keep to the imaginary marriage of Edna and Geoffrey, we may envisage that it is Edna who has died, and Geoffrey who is left. He was fond of Edna but was often irritated at her lack of independence. He regarded himself as an exceedingly sensible and realistic person. His friends think he intellectualizes things too much. He did not weep at the funeral and bore up well through the first period. But after the passing of some time, long or short, the unease, emptiness, sense of loss, yearning, came along, and these emotions confused him greatly. He has no experience of giving way to these feelings, regarding this as womanly weakness. So he might resort to alcohol or tranquillizers. Or perhaps he might become physically ill – for example, get heart disease.

In widowers we do see a small, but statistically significant, increase in mortality from heart disease in the first year after the wife's death. Sometimes Geoffrey will 'solve' the problem by marrying again quickly, often a woman who resembles Edna.

We may guess what his childhood was like. There may have been a major loss, which we know always gives greater vulnerability to losses in adulthood. There may also have been a dismissive attitude to his natural needs for care and love, so that he has learnt that they are an expression of weakness. Thus as a child he, like many other men, has learned to conceal these needs so well that he hardly knows himself that he too has a need for care in order to be able to feel his grief at Edna's death.

The symbiotic relationship

We have here sketched out a couple's relationship in which apparently one is strongly dependent upon the other. In another type of relationship, termed the 'symbiotic relationship', it is more obvious that the dependency is mutual. In its extreme form the couple live only for each other and have a norm that they never quarrel. In some relationships this may be adhered to: 'We have never said a harsh word to each other'. In others quarrels do arise, but they are quickly swept under the carpet and rarely lead to a solution of the problem that started the quarrel. Often there are very few or no friends outside the couple. This type of relationship may exist between spouses, but also between adult children and their parents if they remain living together. It can also be seen in siblings who live together as adults. These are relationships in which one finishes the sentence the other has started saying. They are rarely or never apart. They have almost grown together.

In symbiotic relationships there is great dread of separation. It is our experience that this fear can sometimes be traced back to an unprocessed loss in childhood. If one partner in such a close relationship dies, the other is often at risk of a pathological development of grief, because they feel as if they have lost part of themselves.

Love–hate relationships

A third type of relationship is that marked by love–hate. In this ambivalent relationship the partners live a 'cat-and-dog life' and the relationship is characterized by constant mutual reproaches and bickering. Outsiders often wonder why they do not divorce. If one of the partners in such a relationship dies, we can often see a brief spell of relief, which is succeeded by feelings of emptiness, anxiety and dreariness. The network is seldom ready to accommodate the grief, the sense of loss and the anger. 'She has been grumbling about him every day for the last thirty years, but now that he's dead she's completely cracked up. How can anyone help her?' It can be hard for outsiders to understand the strong attachment there may be between two people who are constantly fighting. It would be too wide-ranging to enter into a deep analysis of the spouses' dynamics. But it is worth noting that in such a relationship there are so many contradictory emotions that the grief work often becomes so complicated that it requires professional help if the bereaved partner is going to get through their grief.

When a child dies

'Losing a child is like losing part of yourself.' That's how most people describe their feelings when they have had to bury a child. This way of putting it is used regardless of whether it is a stillborn baby, a child who is a minor, or a child who is an adult. Some investigations indicate that it is most stressful to lose infants when the natural symbiosis between mother and child is still great. Other investigations show the contrary: that it is particularly stressful to lose older children. Our experience is that losing a child entails very difficult grief work, and that age is of minor importance.

In our society infant mortality is so low that we do not expect to lose our children. We count on their outliving us, and when they do not, it seems to be a breach of the natural order. This has not always been so. We only have to go back a century to find such high infant mortality that a couple had to expect to lose up to half of their children during their lifetime. This expectation, and the fact that people both had more children and were more religious, may explain that a child's death was not nearly such a devastating event as it is today.

Losing a child may result in both avoided and chronic grief. It seems as if it is most often women who end up in a state of chronic grief. They find it hard to let go of the many hopes and dreams that were bound up in the child and thus to complete the fourth task of reinvesting their energy both in other children and in other people. Birthdays and other special anniversaries are particularly difficult. Many parents who have lost a child at birth or during its first year follow this child in their thoughts without this necessarily being pathological grief. They know when it would have started school, when it would have come of age, taken school exams and so on.

It can be hard for some people to understand that the grief over a stillborn baby, even over a miscarriage, can be as great as it often is. For it concerns a child they have not even known.

The Chinese reckon a child's age from its conception, and that expresses an excellent understanding that right from that time the mother begins to get to know her baby and to attach hopes, wishes and dreams to it. Many parents of stillborn or early-dead children are given the well-meant advice to have another baby as quickly as possible. In this way a brake is put on the grief, and the indirect message is given that one baby is just as good as another. Many years ago one of us was working on therapy with a 35-year-old man who had lost a daughter in a cot death. The couple followed the doctors' advice and quickly had another child, a daughter. Not until this daughter was 4 did the man get the necessary help to say farewell to his dead child. When this grief work was over, he exclaimed in surprise: 'But now I can see my youngest daughter in quite a new way!' He could see that she was not identical with the dead daughter. It must be hoped that this grief work meant that the little girl could achieve a more spontaneous and genuine relationship to her father without having to live up to being his notion of someone else.

A child dying is a great strain on a couple's relationship; the grief either brings the parents closer or it makes them drift apart, often resulting in divorce. One of the problems for a couple who lose a child is that the parents often grieve in different ways. The usual thing is that the husband feels he has to be strong to support his grieving wife. He may postpone his grief or show it elsewhere than when he is with his wife. This can result in criticism from the wife that he is not grieving sufficiently or in the right way. The partners often find it hard to accept that they have not suffered the same loss, but that they each had their particular relationship with the dead child, and so they have lost something different. It may also be hard for them to accept that they are not working on the same tasks of grief work at the same time, and that may again lead to mutual criticism. The mother may perhaps be in the midst of her deepest despair (the second task), while the father is at work on the third task and for the first time going to a football match without his dead son. At that point they can only support each other with difficulty, and it is therefore important that they do not rely solely on each other. They both need – separately – to talk to other people about their grief.

If a child has a long illness, the family is forced to spend a lot of time at the hospital and the other children may be neglected. After the death the whole family life has to find a new structure. Many exhausted parents give up, and divorce is sadly often the result.

The third parameter: the mourner's psycho-social circumstances

The network

People who are unable to use their network, or have no network, are at risk when grief strikes them. If someone has nobody to share their thoughts and feelings with, they become anxious and ashamed. If someone does not feel that they have family or friends who understand them, they are threatened with pathological grief. So, as we have shown in the chapter on the four tasks, we spend a lot of time and energy in helping people with a poor network to create support around their grief work.

Risk of isolation

All grief work entails a risk of isolating oneself. Even if someone has a good network, the dislike of 'breaking down' in other people's company may mean that the resources of the network are not used. It is a good sign if a mourner is flexible enough in his grief work both to be able to be alone and with others, according to what is needed.

Being left with young children

There is a widespread misconception that it is a support for a young widow or widower that there are young children to be cared for after the death. On the contrary, young children make such a great emotional and practical demands on the parent who is left, that it is incredibly demanding to have to manage both the children and the grief work. So the family is at risk. Research shows that the young widows are more at risk than older widows. The young widow's despair can be so great that she is not capable of giving the children more than the most superficial practical care and is unable to support the children in their grief. In other cases all the widow's energy is put into coping with the practical matters of being alone and having to see to the children's well-being. So her own grief reaction is neglected. Much preventive work can be done by supporting the lone parent during the first period after the death and by ensuring that they get help both with their own grief work and with supporting the children in their grief. Furthermore, it is often necessary to get grandparents, other family members, friends or children's institutions to give the children extra care in the first six months after the death. It has to be explained that the bereaved parent has not nearly as much to give as before and that the children are therefore extra deprived.

The support that is given financially, practically and emotionally during the first six months can be crucial for whether the new family unit can function harmoniously in the longer term or whether it will turn into a problem family. If a bereaved parent isolates himself/herself with the children, they may end up developing an unhealthy dependence upon the children. Here, the mourner must have support, after some time has passed, to take up activities on their own, so that the children do not find themselves performing the functions of the network.

Sick-leave

Grief work is emotionally very demanding, and it is therefore often necessary for a period to give the bereaved person sick-leave after – for example – the death of a child or a spouse. It is hard to fix a time for how long such sick-leave should last, as there are many factors involved. How demanding is their work? How long are the working hours? Are there important network members at the place of work? What is the attitude of the workplace to showing feelings?

It is our experience that in general there is much too little insight into the amount of psychical energy that is required by grief work. Many general practitioners do not realize the preventive function that an extension of sick-leave may have at the right point of time. A number of our clients have spent an unnecessary amount of energy persuading their doctor that they need to carry on having sick-leave. A sick-leave of four to six weeks has often proved appropriate. Parents who have been left alone with young children usually need a longer period. A long working day is normally much too demanding in the first three to four months after the death. It is fairly common for well-meaning people to urge mourners back to work too early. They assert that it is harmful to stay at home 'brooding over the loss' and that it would be better to get out among other people and 'find something else to think about'. This is usually a misconception. In the first period the mourner needs precisely to be self-absorbed and to turn his attention inward for a large part of the time. The idea that it is best for the grieving person 'to pull himself together and get busy on something else' is very deeply rooted, however.

Cultural and religious support

Mourners who are living in an alien cultural or religious setting do of course feel particularly isolated when crisis or grief strikes them.

Refugees and immigrants who do not have their own countrymen around them therefore need all possible support if they lose a child or spouse. They lack not only a network, but they are also left without the help they can normally find in the religious rites of their homeland. A social worker or GP can therefore provide good support by mediating contact with groups of immigrants who have the same religious background as the mourner. Mobilizing a network that has the right composition is normally an important element of professional crisis help.

However, it is not only immigrants who need attention to see if their network contains the necessary religious help for the mourner. Even within the bounds of a country there are cultural differences in regard to the kind of support the mourner is offered. Someone who has grown up in a religious environment in the country is often let down in an urban society where there is a different attitude to life and death. She may possibly need support in contacting her local parish priest if she is suddenly widowed. In environments where the churches are hardly used this part of a network is often overlooked.

In this parameter – the psycho-social circumstances of the mourner – it is useful to pay attention to rituals. Cultural and religious rites in connection with a death help the mourner to take leave of the departed.

It has been said that the basic humanistic attitude of a culture may be measured by the understanding shown to its mourners. On this view, the urban industrialized society must in general be an unhealthy place to be.

Factors in deciding treatment

We have now surveyed many different factors that are important in identifying who is to have help in

1 avoiding a pathological development of grief;
2 emerging from a delayed, avoided or chronic state of grief.

We have used various examples of how the three parameters separately and together can assist in assessing whether intervention is necessary. But therapists find themselves in two different situations, depending on whether they are asked for help in a relatively acute situation, when the loss or trauma is a natural focus, or whether the client turns to them with problems which do not have their starting-point in the person's grief work.

Acute losses and traumas

GPs, case workers, hospital social workers and psychological consultants are often involved in acute losses and traumas. It may be useful for them to bear the three parameters in mind when assessing whether the grief-stricken person ought to be offered some form of preventive help. However, we would point out that the parameters are only a guide, because the individual client's resources may vary much in composition. So the therapist must above all use his imagination and common sense in applying the parameters.

It is our experience that there is much to be gained by offering acute crisis intervention and grief help. That means it is better to intervene *once too often than once too little*, if there is a suspicion that the client is in the risk group. People who do not wish for outside help usually show this very directly. In Denmark the general problem is not that therapists intervene too much, but rather than they do so too little. There are obvious preventive help measures which are passed over, partly out of a misconceived respect for the natural reaction of grief and crisis, and partly because of lack of knowledge about how to set about giving the help.

Identifying pathological grief development

In 1980 Bowlby wrote that everyone concerned with the treatment of psychological problems will gradually be obliged to recognize the link between neurotic symptoms and pathological grief. We agree wholeheartedly with this attitude, as in our project we have met many clients with anxiety, dreariness, emptiness, guilt, separation anxiety, isolation and incipient abuse of alcohol whom we have been able to help with grief therapy. However, the prerequisite is that therapists begin to be able to identify delayed, avoided and chronic grief when people seek psychological and psychiatric assistance. In the cases in which the grief is mentioned in the initial diagnostic interview, the problem is not so difficult if the parameters are borne in mind.

On the other hand, it is quite a different problem when the loss or trauma is not mentioned. This is fairly common when the client's symptoms are bound up with an avoided state of grief. We therefore consider that one always ought to ask explicitly about losses and traumas when people with mental problems seek help. If it turns out that the client has an important loss in his past life, then we should ask about the circumstances, the attachment and the psycho-social circumstances of the mourner at the time of the loss.

The way in which the 'story' is told can often give a good impression of how the grief work has proceeded. If the client has too few emotions in his description, we must ask about them: for example, to assess whether the emotions are being consciously avoided. If there are many emotions and weeping in the telling of the story, this may indicate a delayed reaction, which has to be taken into account. We see grief reactions that have been delayed for years but which all the time are lying hidden just below the surface. They can then be brought out by merely 'telling the story' to a person who is an 'active listener'.

In the case of chronic grief, one seldom needs to ask the client to tell the story before one discovers how much the loss still fills the person's life. In chronic grief it rather seems as if everything that the mourner recounts is shadowed by the loss. If the mourner cannot go both in and out of their grief and thus sometimes find some relief in the course of the first six months, there is a risk of developing chronic grief. The prognosis for chronic grief is bad, so it is important to intervene before the condition becomes established. Thus there are many grounds for getting clients to tell their story and to describe the loss in detail at the preliminary interview.

However, there are a number of signs which do not necessarily emerge from the 'story' but from the client's symptoms. If we examine the symptoms more closely, it may turn out that the client's depressions always manifest themselves around the anniversary of the death, the birthday or other important dates of the deceased. Some people 'take over' the physical symptoms of the dead person or live in an almost phobic fear of dying from the same disease. When these clients are given help to release their grief, the symptoms disappear.

Grief therapy may also be indicated when a client develops a crisis which is experienced as both incomprehensible and disproportionate when the size of the loss is borne in mind. Thus we have had a number of clients referred to us who have reacted violently to ordinary 'lovers' heartaches'. It has turned out that they have had one or more serious losses in their background when the grief has been avoided. In some cases they have had parents who have committed suicide in their children's adolescence.

It is *always* important to find out *when* the client's symptoms started. If the anxiety, depressions, guilt feelings or alcohol abuse began to develop in connection with the loss or in the years immediately following, that is an indication that one ought to examine how the grief work proceeded after the loss in question.

Those who look after others

There is one risk group we would especially like to draw attention to. This is people who have chosen jobs which entail them taking care of other people's problems and griefs. We are thinking of doctors, nurses, psychologists, social workers and members of similar professions. They belong to a group which is often overlooked, because they are people incredibly good at feeling for everyone else but themselves. From their childhood many of them have been brought up to be 'adult' and responsible. It is they who care for the bereaved in their hour of need. They always appear strong and seem to have everything under control. But all their care for others means that they easily avoid their own emotions.

Particularly in the Student Counselling Service we saw many students who at first sight seemed to function very well, but who had developed symptoms like anxiety and depression without understanding why. It often turned out to derive from unprocessed losses, usually in their childhood, youth or adulthood. As adults they were caught up in a repetition of the pattern of their childhood, feeling that others had greater need of help than they had, and that feelings of others were more important than their own. The consequence of such a pattern is that the ability to enter into the healing grief work as adults is seriously impaired. This is a reminder to therapists to look at their own unprocessed losses before they begin to get involved with grief therapy!

Those at risk of psychoses

People whose psyche is so fragile that their lives are marked by recurrent psychotic states are naturally at risk when losses and traumas shake up their already slender defence mechanisms. This also applies to people who, in pressure situations, teeter on the brink of a psychosis. They are therefore people who ought to have professional help in living through their grief emotions.

We ourselves have no experience of giving crisis or grief help to this group of psychiatric patients, and therefore can express no opinion about the form of treatment that ought to be offered. So we have asked a specialist in psychiatry, Senior Consultant Peder Terpager Rasmussen, to write the following section.

Grief, psychiatry and medical treatment
by Peder Terpager Rasmussen, MD

The nature and classification of psychiatric illnesses is of course not known to many ordinary people who provide their families, friends and neighbours with help in their normal grief reactions, but those who undertake grief therapy for people with pathological grief reactions ought to have some acquaintance with the basic psychiatric disorders and symptoms. But it is equally important for psychiatric staff to be able to distinguish between the normal and the pathological course of grief, including being aware that an acute or more chronic reactive psychosis may be a pathological grief reaction.

It is useful, sometimes even essential, to know the basic psychiatric disorders in order to be able to decide upon any grief treatment that may be offered a person with such a disorder. In the following I shall review the various courses of grief in relation to the most important psychiatric disorders.

Losses come to everyone, regardless of mental health or illness. To me it is striking that the reason that a course of grief has gone awry has often been a conscious, well-meant desire on the part of those around to spare the bereaved person the facts and feelings of the loss. This has so frequently had the opposite effect (that is, it has prolonged the normal process). Mentally ill people, like children, are affected by uncertainty and matters that have been hushed up when they already have an inkling of the true situation. Those around are often under real pressure of time – for instance, should the bereaved person see the dead person before the funeral? – and they have to make a decision. It is my view that, regardless of psychiatric diagnosis, the sick person will justly be able to reproach the therapist if he has not had at least the chance of a final farewell. It will always be an advantage that the bereaved person, regardless of any mental ailment, is informed by someone with whom he has good contact and is attached to, whatever this person's formal position in the family or treatment system may be. Although the decision as to how he or she wishes to be faced with the loss must always remain with the mourner, it is my opinion that at least neurotics and people with a personality disorder ought to be directly encouraged – for example, to see the dead person – whereas we should probably be more hesitant in this respect with psychotics, and, when the decision is made, the person should be given support in their farewell to the deceased. If the bereaved person is in doubt, the doubt ought to benefit the grief process.

Acute reactive psychosis with confusion and disorientation about (for instance) time and place combined with loss of memory may be regarded as a kind of 'protection' against recognition of the loss and may affect normal personalities when the trauma is sufficiently severe and dramatic – or affect frail personalities when there have been minor or repeated traumas. The state may be regarded as a kind of unconscious refusal to assume the first task of the grief process: recognition of the loss (see Chapter Two). As a rule these states require acute psychiatric admission and the relevant treatment will often be medical with drugs of the neuroleptic or benzodiazepine group (see below). Close contact, preferably in the form of permanent supervision, is a great advantage in these short-term situations when the patient is in severe distress and the content of the trauma is often gradually beginning to emerge into his consciousness. It is important that the therapist dares to follow up the patient's own tentative approaches, without the therapist being confrontational beyond what the psychotic or recently psychotic patient paves the way for himself. These patients often rapidly become non-psychotic and then have a need for help in clarifying and processing the content of the trauma (see page 29).

Hallucinations are normally taken as a clearly psychotic feature and may be seen in persons with reactive psychoses, but often at the beginning of an otherwise normal course of grief there may be, for example, auditory hallucinations (the dead person's footsteps or voice), without this necessarily having to be viewed as a psychotic feature or to frighten those around. Illusions in which the bereaved person misinterprets real sense impressions (for example, imagines he recognizes the deceased from behind in a crowd) are also often found soon after the death, and ought not to frighten family and friends, but should be seen as a sign that the person has not fully recognized the loss.

Reactive psychoses with depressive content in connection with losses will often be longer-lasting and less violent. There may be both acute and pathological course of grief, and these ought to be processed as such. Finally, what are known as endogenous depressions (those coming from within), with special bodily depressive symptoms like early-morning waking, diurnal variation (often worst in the morning), dry mouth, constipation, reduced psycho-motor rate and often quite exaggerated guilt feelings, may be engendered by a trauma. The state is also called a psycho-provoked endogenous depression and has its own typical course. The treatment ought here to be primarily biological with anti-depressants or electro-convulsive therapy (ECT). The trauma should not be processed before the psychotic depression has been relieved.

Delayed grief, in which several years after the trauma the patient only needs space and minimum help before he himself sees the benefit of processing his loss and has an urge to do so in the relevant emotional way, should be supported regardless of the psychiatric diagnosis.

The avoided grief reaction, in which in an almost phobic way the bereaved person consciously avoids a number of situations or places which elicit the feelings of grief, is most often seen in people with a neurotic or disordered personality. As already mentioned, the treatment consists of a very active confrontation with the avoided emotions and it must therefore always be expected that the patients will be experienced as worse during this treatment which – in order to function at all – requires the patient to be free of drugs and alcohol. So this treatment ought not to be initiated with people who are so frail that they cannot tolerate becoming emotionally overwhelmed; that is, patients close to psychosis or those with several suicide attempts behind them. Thus it will be wrong to initiate this form of treatment with either manic depressives or schizophrenics.

Clear dementia will likewise be a contra-indication, when the patient both may become more confused and also can scarcely hold on to the content of the therapy (see also page 157).

Abuse of both medicine and drugs, particularly benzodiazepines, makes treatment impossible. There must be clear contracts about being free of drugs and possibly a periodic Antabuse treatment for these patients before therapy is commenced.

Personality disorders are not in themselves a contra-indication, but the personality and circumstances must be assessed in each individual case.

Chronic grief may be regarded as holding on to the grief and to the content of life, possibly status, which the grief gives to the mourner, or perhaps just as often a fear of the problems which will make themselves felt if the person has to cope with his own life without the deceased. As chronic grief is most often seen in neurotic people and not in those at risk of psychoses, there is no reason to hold back. But one should be aware that, through diagnostic uncertainty, one may come to pressurize an endogenous depressive too strongly, resulting in an experience of defeat and sense of inadequacy and thus increased risk of suicide. The diagnostic assessment ought in these cases, as far as possible, to be made by professionals who are familiar with both pathological grief reactions and classical psychiatry. Where there is doubt about the diagnosis, one should primarily give anti-depressant treatment in a relevant dosage and for a relevant period and, once this has produced no result, embark on psychotherapy, which is demanding for both patient and therapist.

Drug treatment in grief states

> When Mama is ill, she is given medicine; Mama's being given medicine, so she's ill.
>
> *- Freely after Holberg*

In normal acute as well as pathological grief states, one frequently sees a number of psychical symptoms like anxiety, restlessness, depressive thoughts, lack of appetite and sleeping difficulties. The symptoms, along with a number of physical disorders, may easily give both the patient and the doctor the impression that there is illness involved, and the link to a past or recent loss is not always realized, which may often lead to unnecessary or sometimes harmful treatment with drugs. It must be made clear once and for all that the processing of a loss is done by confronting realities and emotions, and that a grief process can *never* be lived through on a prescription.

In the first critical days of a grief process, sleeping-pills may, however, be necessary in order to secure the physical and mental restitution that is necessary for getting through the crisis. But tranquillizers like benzodiazepines or neuroleptics, which inhibit or prevent the emotional confrontation with the content of the grief and thus the course of the grief process, are regarded as contra-indicated, as at best they prolong the process, at worst 'freeze' it, with a rising need for 'anaesthesia' with drugs or alcohol as a result. So-called 'support medicine' ought thus to be avoided. It entails turning the grieving person into a sick case, and this can, in the longer term, lead to a pathological grief reaction.

I shall here briefly review the three most relevant main groups of psycho-active drugs and their use. For more detailed information about any particular preparation, we may refer to the comprehensive list of drugs which can be found in most libraries or given by the prescribing doctor.

If a grieving person is being given drug treatment, the grief helper or therapist along with the patient ought to contact the treating doctor with a view to discussing the necessity of this and the possibility of giving it up.

Benzodiazepines

These preparations are used as tranquillizers, anxiolytics and hypnotics. There are minor differences in preparations, but the main effect is the same; namely, tranquillizing in small doses and hypnotic in larger doses. As already mentioned, during the first days after a loss it may be possible to secure a night's sleep with such preparations, but they have no healing effect in themselves and ought therefore to be avoided so as not to delay or interrupt an otherwise natural course of grief. Active grief treatment of a pathological grief reaction ought therefore not to be initiated unless there is a clear contract between patient and therapist about total freedom from drugs, possibly after gradual withdrawal.

Neuroleptics or major tranquillizers

These anti-psychotic drugs have a normalizing effect on psychoses and, at low dosage, a generally tranquillizing effect on non-psychotic persons. They should only be used with psychotic patients and never as treatment for a grief reaction. In people with psychoses or borderline psychosis prior to a loss, it must be a specialist assessment whether the medication can or ought to be changed in the course of grief.

Anti-depressants

These preparations often have a good effect on depression of what is known as the endogenous (coming from within, manic-depressive) type.

In the nature of things, to differentiate between endogenous depression, reactive depression, psycho-provoked endogenous depression and pathological or normal grief reaction is often difficult. As anti-depressants are only effective for the endogenous types, which on the other hand may be made worse by psychotherapy, it will be wise in cases of doubt to carry out a drug treatment according to the rules and then, if there has been no effect after about two months, to commence grief therapy. Since anti-depressants are generally regarded as not so emotion-inhibiting as benzodiazepines and neuroleptics, I consider that it may sometimes be defensible to maintain the anti-depressant treatment during a course of grief therapy.

Chapter four

Crisis intervention and grief therapy in a group setting

The central theme running through this book is the method of working in 'the open grief group'. We have shown how in the group we help clients with acute, delayed, avoided and chronic grief. As it is largely individual therapy in a group, it will also be possible to use most of the methods we have mentioned so far in individual treatment. In this chapter we shall describe how we developed the group method and we shall review the particular methods that are employed in the open grief group.

When we teach, there are three questions which we always have to answer. How can a group provide the security required for people to have the courage to unlock the pain and anger of their grief? How can mourners who have to use almost all their energy in mastering their own grief, manage to find room for other people's grief as well? How can the group give the mourner a sense of having a network, when new members are constantly joining and others are leaving? The concerns that lie behind these questions are the same ones we had before we adopted the method.

As we have mentioned, for about ten years we have both been engaged with various forms of group therapy and have thus had thorough experience of the advantages and limitations of working with therapeutic groups. In different ways each of us had also worked with losses and traumas and so had some training in the methods of crisis intervention both in individual treatment and in groups.

In 1980 we met the Canadian-Dutch professor Ron Ramsay. For many years he had been specializing in the treatment of symptom-producing avoided grief reactions. The losses had to be more than two years back in time. His work of eliciting the healing emotional grief reaction to the loss was done in individual short-term treatment of six to eight sessions spread over some weeks. His technique was confrontational in order to evoke and hold on to the emotions until the fear of the emotions had died away. The clients then had contact with the necessary pain and anger, so that they could continue their grief work on their own with help from their network.

Ramsay's frame of reference was that of behaviour therapy. He sees the avoided grief as a result of an almost phobic fear of strong and painful emotions. The avoidance is so massive that it requires a therapist-controlled situation to break it. As with phobias, the client has to be held to the task of living through the scaring emotions. Ramsay saw acute, delayed and avoided grief reactions as a hierarchic system in which access to the emotions becomes less and less open.

Ramsay's intensely confrontational method is dramatic. So the idea came to us that it would be possible to break down the defence against the emotions of grief more gently if these people were gathered into a group. We presumed that the clients would become less afraid of their emotions if they saw other people living through their pain and finding relief by letting go. We also knew that being able to use a network is part of the healing process. So we supposed that the group would function as a network which could give a different kind of care and support from that which an individual therapist can provide. Finally, the shared focus on losses and traumas would perhaps make it easier to stress the universally human and healthy aspect of the grief process.

In the autumn of 1980 we gathered the first three clients, who quite soon expressed relief at being there with other people who had suffered losses. One was working on a sister's suicide, another on the death of her father when the client was an adolescent and another on a traumatic divorce one year before.

Now, ten years later, we are surprised at the misgivings we had before starting. Good results with the 900 or so clients we have worked with in an open grief group have confirmed our view that in an effective and gentle way the group supports healthy grief work.

In the following we want to describe how the group is used and thereby answer the three questions mentioned by way of introduction. The individual work in the group is shown by the survey of the four tasks of grief work and was further amplified in Chapter Two.

The grief group as a network

'A joy shared is a double joy, a sorrow shared is half a sorrow.' This old adage expresses the essence of grief work in a group. To be able to share one's feelings with others is crucial for all personal growth. So there can hardly be any doubt that many grieving people could benefit from being in a grief group for a while.

It is our experience that the most difficult and most vulnerable time after a death comes after three to four months. By this time the mourner is beginning to make contact with the final farewell. This brings a frightening emptiness, which often coincides with the person's network beginning to withdraw, because the new 'everyday life' has begun. A grief group can be a great help at this point.

In England for many years self-help organizations have been developed for people with serious losses, so that mourners can find support in a self-help group when their private network falls short. Some groups are especially for parents who have lost children, others for widows and widowers. The principle of these grief groups is to strengthen the network around the bereaved person, the same line of reasoning which made us begin working with a therapeutic group. A similar development is taking place in Denmark.

However, the group we are describing is an option offered to people who without professional help may risk developing pathological grief. In the therapist-guided group it is possible to use the network idea in such a way that the healthy forces in the grief process are highlighted. The group members can almost always see the healing power that comes when others feel pain and anger, even though they themselves may be finding it hard to let go of their emotions. It is our experience that this focusing on health instead of illness is more difficult in individual treatment.

Sometimes people may be afraid of going mad with grief. Their fear may be reinforced if they often see the dead person in front of them. A therapist will be able to calm them by saying that this is a quite usual part of the healthy grief process. But it is much more effective if another member of the group says, 'That is just what happened to me three months ago. Now I'm not afraid of going mad any more, even though I still sometimes see my husband at home.' Even the most persuasive therapist cannot compete with the force that lies in a statement from somebody who has just lived through a similar process.

Some of the people who live with unreleased grief feel that if they once begin to weep, they will not be able to stop the tears. In the group they witness time and time again that those who give way to their tears are only able at a maximum to cry for ten to fifteen minutes. The body is then so relaxed that the weeping stops by itself.

These examples show how the grief group provides a framework for the grief work which an individual treatment cannot give. A person weeps on his own account and with others in the grief group. The person who is weeping over the loss of a spouse may unleash the weeping of someone who is nursing the loss of their baby. The person who is grieving over the loss of a father or mother can influence someone who, as a 12-year-old, lost his father or mother and who has never felt the pain of this loss, because at that time nobody could accommodate the child's feelings.

Sandra (see Chapter Two) wrote the following about the group as a network:

> However different we all doubtless are in our everyday lives, this loss/grief of ours has brought us together. We have cursed and sworn, wept and suffered together, it has been incredible to experience. Although our griefs are different, the reactions, the emotions around it are amazingly similar. It has been a tremendous help to know that one is not alone.

The atmosphere of the grief group

For most people the group develops into a refuge where there is room for all emotions and where help is to be found in understanding the often confusing process that grief work can be. We have mentioned several times that healthy grief work is a process in which one grasps the emotions of grief in order to be able to let go of them again. The group's atmosphere has been proved to support this process.

We can still be amazed that at one moment the clients can come up the stairs into the group room enjoying a chat, and fifteen minutes later perhaps four of them are weeping and one is sobbing deeply. It seems as if they create a space around them which, combined with the security which our presence gives, makes it possible to throw off the controls. Of course this makes our work far easier. We have the atmosphere as a catalyst, and often just a few sympathetic remarks from us are enough for the emotions to be released. Correspondingly, this space allows room for much genuine laughter and gaiety. In just a few minutes the mood may change from liberating bursts of laughter into deep seriousness. These emotional fluctuations are to us a demonstration that it is life-giving to be able to go in and out of the emotions of grief.

It is usual that, in the latter part of their course, clients come just to be present in the group. They spend a couple of minutes telling how they are. They do not want any help from us – just need to be in the 'atmosphere' and perhaps gather some strength for their pathway onward.

During some periods there are themes which recur in several members, just because they influence one another. For some weeks there is much anger in the group; in others pain is the dominant factor. One theme may be guilt – for example, at not feeling the loss so much any more, now that they are feeling better. Another theme may be bitterness, in which group members can help one another to separate the bitterness into anger and pain. One meeting may be very emotional, at which nearly everyone weeps; another may be marked by the third task, with much concentration on meeting new challenges. The group members inspire one another into new ways of understanding their own pathway and new ways of dealing with difficulties. When one person has managed to write an important letter to the deceased and has read it aloud to the group, someone else will have much less resistance to undertaking the same task. When one person has succeeded in asking a member of his family for help and has met with a good response, it is easier to get someone else to do something similar. Thus some valuable group norms develop about daring to show feelings and assuming new challenges even when the pain is great.

There is a need for much care to be shown to those clients who have to have support with the second task, the deep pain. As we sit on cushions on the floor, we can easily arrange ourselves so that the weeper is either given a supporting arm round them or sits close to someone else. Often it is the clients who spontaneously put an arm round the weeper. Sometimes we move a trainee over to the client to offer her proximity. It has often amazed us that clients will so confidingly nestle up to a trainee whom they have seen only a couple of times before and who rarely says anything in the group. We take that as a sign of how strong is the need for bodily closeness and warmth when we grieve.

We often ourselves put an arm around a client, but we seldom use greater bodily proximity. We have experimented a good deal with this, because at the beginning we believed that body contact was a task we should undertake. But we discovered that the clients can just as well use the trainees or each other, which is better training in using a network. In individual treatment, of course, the therapist has to offer physical contact herself.

Framework of the grief group

The group meets twice a week, two hours with the therapists and one hour alone over a cup of coffee afterwards. The frequency makes it possible to sustain the intense atmosphere and makes the time between the meetings bearable for those members who are in a phase in which the pain is severe. We therefore encourage the clients to come twice a week for the first months. Then it is usual to come once a week for a period, and later drop to once a fortnight. Towards the end of the course, many prefer to have a break for a little time to try out whether they have got so far in their grief work that they can manage the rest themselves. In this way the final goodbye to the group is prepared for over some time.

Thus the clients move from a very close, intense involvement in the group to a looser link. This should not be taken to mean that in reality the group members can come and go as they please. We have definite arrangements with each one as to how frequently they come, and if someone cannot attend a meeting as agreed, they must phone to say so. But group members who are having a break know that they always can come if they need to. Group members who stay away without giving word are contacted, usually after they have missed a couple of times.

All the time the work in the group has a therapeutic aim and a focus that is maintained by the therapists. There is no room for chatter about problems that are not related to the grief work. So it is important for their sense of being a group that over the coffee, in the absence of the therapists, there is opportunity to relax and talk about other problems. Often there is further talk about what has gone on in the group. New and uncertain clients are welcomed into the fellowship. There is mutual support and the giving of good advice. Sometimes members make arrangements to contact one another between meetings. This informal socializing thus functions as a temporary network twice a week. For a number of clients this is their first experience of how a network can be used. Farewell letters to the group show again and again how important this feeling of fellowship has been to the individual. So we always stress to new members that the coffee time is just as important a part of the therapy as the time spent with us.

The open grief group

As we have said, the group is open. That means that new clients are regularly joining while others stop coming. It is most common for a group course to last three to four months. Some people find help in just a few visits; others are attached to the group for a year or so. During the period when clients come to the group only rarely, it acts as a kind of safety net. Many people feel that they are better able to cope with the pain and the many new challenges if they know that they can always find help in the group should things become too fraught. Together with the client we assess when it is time to stop coming. This process will be described later in this chapter.

Being an open group also means that the clients are at various stages in their grief process, and this itself is crucial for the success of the method. Some of them are new and hesitant. Others are dominated by the emotions of their grief. Others again are focusing mainly on acquiring skills in order to cope with their new way of life, and the final farewell therefore seems to be within reach. This structure shows the development of healthy grief work in a natural way. It gives hope to see other people daring to enter into their pain and to hear at the next group meeting how it brought them relief in the days that followed. When someone has just begun their grief work, it gives them hope to see those who have got to the stage where they can go in and out of the emotions of grief and undertake new challenges. The newcomers experience that it is possible to have many good hours and, in the course of time, days, despite the loss and the pain. For about a year we had two mothers in the group whose children had been killed. Paradoxically, the difficult grief work of these two women gave many of the others hope. 'If those two can get as far as being able to believe in a future, and if they dare to process their great grief towards a final farewell, then I ought to be able to as well,' was the theme that recurred in many farewell letters of that period.

Assimilation into the group

The new group member meets many unfamiliar faces. At each group meeting there are between six and twelve participants and along with us also a couple of doctors, psychologists, or social workers under training. So there are many people to whom the group member has to relate. At the admission interview the new client is therefore briefed that at the first meeting there is freedom just to be present at the group and to decide afterwards whether he wishes to use the grief group.

At the meeting, the newcomer is introduced with a brief round of names, each person giving his own name. Sometimes the group members add a couple of sentences about the kind of loss or trauma they are working on in the group. After that, the newcomer can lean back and form an impression of how the group works. As we have said, the atmosphere in the group is usually very intense and emotionally charged, and it is therefore a powerful experience for most people just to be there. That also applies to the new trainees, by the way.

Just before the group finishes up after two hours, the newcomer is asked what it was like to be in the group. Has he or she recognized anything of their own grief work and will they be coming to the next meeting? As a rule, one or more events in the group have affected the newcomer, who therefore feels an urge to tell the others about the loss or trauma that has brought him to the group. The speaking of these words almost always means an acceptance of the group and a wish to go on coming. We also ensure that the new attenders will stay and have coffee with the others. We know from experience that the clients are the best people to convince a newcomer that the group is a secure and good place to be. A client who has been overwhelmed by the intensity of his first group meeting will be supported by the others, who felt just the same at first, but who now feel helped by the emotional openness.

A few people need to come along to the group several times before they can decide whether they wish to make use of it. For instance, a mother who had lost her child came to the group six times before she made the final decision. Each time we got her to tell how it affected her to be in the group and of her misgivings about sharing her despair with the others. Beyond that, we put our trust in the process in the group. We reckoned that it would gradually make her less afraid both of her own and other people's feelings, and that the socializing after the group would help to motivate her. We hoped that the healthy part of her would develop by seeing how the others used the group in their grief work. We expected this process to give her the necessary push into slowly daring to break with her emotion-inhibiting pattern. At the sixth meeting she decided to tell the group in detail how her child died. She began to weep in the midst of the story, and a trainee put an arm caringly around her. For a moment she let herself go, and the weeping meant that for the first time since her child's death she felt some easing of her grief. After that, she decided to use the group.

The role of the therapists in the grief group

The therapists play a very directive role in the group, because the focus must be kept on the bereavement and the four tasks of grief work. As we have mentioned, the interventions have the character of individual treatment in a group. The clients take turns to contribute. Some need a lot of time, others mention only tasks they have planned to carry out before the next session. But each meeting everyone is expected to say how they are faring.

Usually the clients start out by telling how they have felt since last time, or how a particular task has been handled. On this basis, it is assessed what interventions would be appropriate. Sometimes the group's response is brought in: 'What is your reaction to what Lise has to say?' On other occasions a particular client, who it is known has or has had a problem similar to Lise's, is asked: 'Have you got any advice for Lise?'

Despite the directive form, the other group members are far from passive while the work concentrates on the individual. It is characteristic that almost everything that is spoken about in the group awakens an echo in most members. Just because grief work always consists of the same constituent processes, the clients recognize themselves in one another – and often one client's work will set another going. It is the therapist's task to support this.

A dramatic example was when Emma, whose husband had hanged himself after many years' stressful illness, gave vent to the feeling of relief she had felt in the midst of her grief. The severe stress of many years was over when her husband died, but this feeling of relief felt so forbidden that she had avoided it. Emma wept when she was finally able to talk about her relief, but Susanne wept even more vehemently; her husband had also died after a long, severe illness four years before. Susanne's only grief reaction had hitherto been intense anger. Emma's courage in facing up to her relief became a decisive help to Susanne. It meant a turning-point in her grief work. Susanne wept after this at many meetings over daring to feel relief at her husband's death. Ultimately, the opening meant that she could later feel the pain at having lost the husband she once had loved and with whom she had had a warm and good relationship before the illness. The example of Emma and Susanne is typical of how the group members can use each other in their grief work.

It is the therapist's responsibility to exploit and support these opportunities in the group. It is therefore essential for there to be two therapists in such a group. Awareness must be directed not only towards individual grief therapy or grief-crisis help, but also towards the process of the group, so that a Susanne and an Emma can use each other in the best way possible. Therapists must therefore have some knowledge of group processes and of group therapy before they start working with therapeutic grief groups.

The relationship between clients and therapists in the grief group

Many people will probably immediately imagine that, with the great intensity of emotion in the group, there will be a very strong dependency on the therapists. It is indeed true that they are important for the clients while they are in the group, but the farewell letters show again and again that the strong attachment is to the group as a whole, not just to the therapists.

As a therapist a person needs authority. The clients have to feel understood and supported by the therapists, and this gives the trusting contact that is necessary for the interventions to succeed. It regularly happens that a client gets angry with the therapist. In this case, opportunity must be given for the anger to be expressed. If a mistake has been made, this must of course be acknowledged to the client.

In our grief group the clients conceive us more as a team than as individuals. Often they ascribe a remark made by one to the other. We never correct them. We are well content to be regarded as an entity. But some clients do attach themselves more to one than the other. Often this attachment takes place at the preliminary interview and it may last for the whole course of the group. This means that this therapist's words have a little more weight than the other's, and we exploit that when difficult matters have to be raised.

Sometimes we make use of the fact that there are two of us by adopting opposite points of view. Often a client is in a dilemma. One side of the client wants to get started on the third task – daring to do something new; the other side is afraid and digs in its heels. In such a situation one of us will support the courageous side and press the client to take on a fear-provoking task that is more closely defined; for instance, to contact a person in the network. The other will support the client's anxious side and assert that the client is hardly ready to take on such a task yet. In this way the client is given the chance of seeing his dilemma played out between us and so can choose more freely. Often the client chooses to undertake the difficult task.

Taking leave of the grief group

As the whole basic theme in this group is to bid farewell to something important, it is natural that we make much of saying goodbye to the group. As we have said, we often let the clients taper off their attendance, but it would run counter to the principles of the group just to let their membership fade away. So we fix the final date in consort with the client. It may be hard to decide that one is ready to manage on one's own with one's network. If the loss is a recent one, the client will still be having a lot of ups and downs at that particular time, and he or she knows that it may be one or more years yet before they have got through their grief work. They know that one never becomes the same person again that one was before the loss, but one hopes to become a stronger and wiser person. The clients may feel a temptation to stay in the security that the group affords, but the great majority of them know within themselves when the time has come to let go of the group. They witness the many new members with strong grief reactions, and that makes their own progress noticeable. So it feels right to them to try their strength outside the group. For clients with old traumas or delayed or avoided grief, it is often easier to make the decision to leave the group. Their course has been shorter, and they get so much new strength from their grief work that the group more rapidly fades in importance.

Some clients attempt to avoid the final leave-taking by staying away. We contact them and put pressure upon them to fix a date for a farewell, because we regard this farewell as a very important part of the process. This may happen with clients whose course of attendance at the group has proceeded satisfactorily in our view, as well as with clients who seem to be finishing too early.

Two rituals are linked to saying goodbye to the group. One is the reading out of a farewell letter. The other is that the leaver has to say goodbye to each individual group member and to the therapists. In the second ritual we lay stress on the clients using the word 'Goodbye', not just 'Cheers' or 'Be seeing you'.

The clients work on the goodbye letter for varying lengths of time. It must contain an assessment of what it has meant to them to be in the group and a farewell. The letters are often very varied and moving. Most of them express that the strongest experience has been the close human fellowship where they have felt both more naked and more secure than ever before. Often a new faith in human fellowship springs up out of the group experience. There may be grief at not having the opportunity to use the many new human experiences with the dead person and a sadness that it had to be the loss itself that was to bring about the sense of personal growth.

The farewell letters are composed very variedly. Some are brief and pithy, others are long and detailed. We shall here quote one to give an impression of both the breadth and depth.

Dear Nini and Marianne, and all of the others of you in the group,

The time to say goodbye has come. In this quiet evening hour I am sitting with the picture of Martin and Jannie in front of me, and what is more natural than that the tears are welling up out of the corners of my eyes? Tears that tell of the enormous gap left by Martin and Jannie, tears at having to say goodbye to all of you, who have meant so much to me.

It is more or less a year and a half since I started – yes, started from the bottom. I could compare myself with a little newborn child who is completely helpless. If only I were adult enough to be able to manage for myself, but the spark had got lost, the light had gone out – I had no zest for life; without your help I would, perhaps not literally, be dead, my body would probably have gone on living, but my inner self would have been dead.

I remember so clearly the first time I sat down here on the blue cushions, I was stiff and apathetic, probably a bit afraid of what all this was. Could I use any of it for anything? A thought went through me. But who can help me? I shall never become a human being again, my two little children are dead, I want to have them again, nobody can give them back to me, so there is no help to be had. As you can understand, I felt that just then I had nothing to live for.

Slowly, time after time, all of you sitting here, along with all those who stopped coming in the course of time, have gradually pulled me up. It has been a long, hard and difficult process to have to go through, but when I now sit here and think back, there must somewhere have been a little will to live left in me, for it is clear that, if I hadn't done anything about it myself, your help might have been wasted.

Many emotions have been touched, and I have written a number of letters. The letters to the children are probably the most important ones for me. I remember that when I read them out I put the pictures of Martin and Jannie down in front of me, I really felt that they were there right before me, a feeling that was both nice and nasty, nice in the sense that I managed to say in words that they were both wanted children, and nasty because, when they were there so close to me, they were not two little living people who could be given a proper hug.

Your understanding of the feelings which at that time I had towards Peter (I am thinking of when I missed him more than I hated him) has been quite an indescribable help to me. At that time it was all just chaos to me, and at times I asked myself whether I was really quite sane. I tried to talk to the family about all these feelings, but I found no understanding there, they just flung at me, 'Think of what he has done', and I had an even worse conscience about not just hating him. The support you gave me, when you said, 'The one thing does not exclude the other, obviously you don't forget the good years you had together' – that was a fantastic help to me. I am glad today, when I have got to the point of being able to say that I only hate him, I do not miss him at all, this step I think has been very important to me, for with it I have said goodbye to the past and hallo to the future.

What the future holds I do not know, thank heaven, but tragic events may happen to me again, but whatever may happen, I believe that with this experience I have now, I can better understand how to tackle the situation. Of course I hope that there are some good years in store for me, that the animal we all know here, that lives in us, will scratch at the wound less and less. The gap left by Martin and Jannie will always be there, they will always be a part of me, always fill part of my heart. I am not afraid of my own death, for I hope and believe that my two little children will be standing on the other side with arms outstretched to welcome me.

I have got to the bitter end, where the letter has to be wound up, and that means that I have to say goodbye to all of you. To all of you in the group. You have meant so much to me. You have been part of my life and will remain so, for I shall never forget you. I wish you all the best.

To you, Nini and Marianne: thank you for picking me up and, not least, thanks for the valuable place you fill here. I shall never forget you. I shall miss you all, even though I know that it is the right thing for me to say goodbye to you today. Goodbye.

Chapter five

Eleven examples of crisis intervention and grief therapy

In this chapter we shall survey eleven courses of treatment. Therapists should be able to find inspiration here to intervene in *acute crisis*, *delayed* and *avoided grief*. An example of a client with chronic development of grief whose grief therapy we were unable to complete shows why the outlook is poor when the grief has become chronic. Also, *alcohol abuse* is discussed, which is a difficult problem in grief therapy, because the grieving person is accustomed to avoid his emotions with the aid of alcohol. We have therefore chosen to give an example of how we had to abandon grief therapy with a female alcoholic and how another course of grief therapy with an alcoholic was successful, among other things because we got the client through the grief work involved in saying farewell to 'his best friend', namely, alcohol.

Before we describe the work of treatment, we shall outline the qualifications required for working with grief and crisis.

What is required of therapists

The therapist must be able to create psychological space around the client in which a deep understanding for the pain can be felt and in which there is respect for the difficulty of giving way and feeling the bereavement and the despair. It is hard to describe how this space is created. There is a delicate balance between ability to empathize, technical know-how and timing.

In therapeutic work the therapist's personality is a significant factor. The ability to empathize is necessary for making the contact with the client which is the basis of the co-operation. In crisis intervention and grief therapy it is important to be able to convey one's understanding for the client's situation both verbally and non-verbally. When the client feels understood, then a sense of security arises, which makes it possible for the therapist to be both confrontational and caring.

Some therapists have natural abilities. Their whole personality radiates calm, security and authority. Most others can, through teaching, training and supervision, learn to create the necessary space around the client.

However, it is not enough to be able to create confidence and security. Getting a client into contact with the emotions of grief also requires a broad view and practical know-how. Thus one must be able to choose words and sentences which confront the client with his loss. In connection with our discussion of the first task (pages 33–6), we gave examples of how we used words like 'alone', 'single parent', 'never again', 'John isn't coming back again, he is dead, it is past' in connection with divorce and a death. They are words and phrases which affect the awareness, and therefore pave the way for the emotions of grief. One can *learn* to use well-chosen words with the right emotional content, although to a beginner it often feels brutal to have to be so confrontational.

It is also important that voice control is used consciously. A much too loud, matter-of-fact quality of voice creates just as much resistance in the client as does an over-sugary voice. The voice has to be used as a kind of sounding-board for the client's emotions. It should radiate calm, strength and sympathy. The client has to feel that 'there is one person present who has the breadth of vision and strength to be able to understand and accommodate my feelings'.

Some therapists become so touched by the often tragic stories of their clients that they naturally and quietly weep with the clients. Most clients are able to use this visible compassion on the therapist's part. Of course the emotions must not be allowed to block the therapist's broad view, and she must not weep so violently that the client feels she has to console the therapist.

The therapist's own attitude to grief work is important. If we are to convince our clients that the necessary pain contains a healthy process, we have to believe this ourselves. It is a great help to the clients if we can explain to them in simple words the healing forces to be found in their tears and anger. Fear, shame and guilt feelings can be reduced if the clients understand that grief is health and not illness.

A natural consequence of this is that the therapist must have worked through his own grief in order to be able to help others with theirs. In this, as in all other therapeutic work, the therapist's own 'blind spots' will inhibit the client's healing process. In other words, a therapist will rarely be able to help a client further with the work of the four tasks than he himself has got with his own losses. When the above requirements have been met, most therapists will be able both to give crisis intervention and to provide crisis and grief help in cases of new or delayed grief without major complications.

When more complicated delayed grief reactions and avoided or chronic grief development are involved, the form of treatment is grief therapy. It requires psychotherapeutic training and experience of emotionally confrontational methods to be able to carry out grief therapy.

Making contracts

Before we begin a course of grief therapy, the client has to know what is involved. He must realize that the focus of the treatment will be the bereavement and the process through which the grieving person has to pass in order to be 'whole' again. He has to understand that problems that are not linked to the loss will be ignored – see Sandra's therapy, where we concentrated the treatment on her mother's death and did not concern ourselves with her problems at work. In other words, we make a contract with the client to work on the grief. This contract is necessary, because the therapist is so directive, and because the emotions that come out during the therapy may be fairly violent.

It may be useful for the client to understand that in grief therapy the client and the therapist are working together as a team. They have a commitment to each other. The therapist commits himself to make available all his knowledge and experience as well as the stipulated time. Telephone hours during which the client can get hold of the therapist outside the therapy also have their place, but must not be abused, as the client may be tempted to use the therapist as a network, instead of cultivating his own. The client promises to attend a certain number of times. Thus he must not stay away in mid-course, when the pain is increasing.

In group treatment, the clients also have an obligation to be together and to support one another for an hour after each group session.

We regard 'playing an open hand' as an important element in grief therapy, because it often makes this difficult process less intimidating. We explain how normal grief work proceeds and how we all have mental strength to get through the grief, if only we have the courage to use it. It is our experience that this instruction makes it easier for the clients to understand and thus accept the component contracts which we are constantly making with them. Often these have to do with homework assignments between sessions. Letter-writing is a typical example of a contract. A boundary-breaching meeting with a network person may be another kind of contract. In the description of the course of treatment there are many examples of such component contracts.

Suicide contracts

It is very common for someone to have thoughts of suicide when they have to get through a great grief. It may therefore be necessary to have a suicide contract with the client.

In the diagnostic interview, we always ask about the client's thoughts of suicide. It is important to ask straight out: 'Do you have thoughts which frighten you?', 'Do you think of doing yourself any harm or committing suicide?', 'Are you afraid you might carry out these thoughts?' The commonest thing is that the mourner is thinking of taking his own life, and knows deep down that he will not actually do it.

If the client has suicidal thoughts, one ought always to make what may be called a suicide contract. This is an agreement that so long as he is under treatment he will not attempt suicide. We explain that such a contract is necessary if we are going to offer help. It can give the security we need to be able to help the client through his pain. We stress that he is welcome to talk about his urge to suicide in the group, but that he must not carry out any suicidal acts.

The suicide contract is not only reassuring for the therapist but for the client too. It strengthens that side of him which wants to get through the pain and go on living.

It sometimes happens that we have to remind the clients of the contract during the treatment, if the thoughts are asserting themselves again. Suicide usually coincides with depression. It is therefore hardly surprising that the mourner is most threatened when the bereavement entails emptiness, anxiety and a tense and defeatist attitude to the future, which fill the client in a pathetically 'dead' way.

In the ten years we have been working with the open grief group, we have not had one suicide among the clients, but we have very often talked to them about their thoughts and feelings at no longer being able to cope with life.

So all workers with people in crisis and grief ought, if they feel unsure, to obtain a suicide contract with their clients. It is reassuring to both parties, because we know that the necessary pain at the beginning of the course of treatment can make the mourner feel a growing need to escape. When the grieving person begins to be able to release his grief by, for example, being able to have a good cry, it is common to see that the will to live returns, even though the struggle is hard and distressing for a long time.

Survey of the chosen examples

The eleven courses of treatment are divided up according to the kind of grief reaction: *acute crisis reaction, delayed grief, avoided grief* and *chronic grief.*

Crisis help, grief help and crisis intervention

1 Two women whose bereavements were so great that their networks were unable to accommodate them (help in the first and second tasks).
2 A man afflicted by a traumatic experience which brought about a crisis state with attacks of anxiety and insomnia (second and third tasks).
3 A man with several bereavements and with no network (second task).

Grief therapy for delayed grief

1 A woman with six months' delayed grief reaction after her husband's traumatic illness and death (second, third and fourth tasks).
2 A woman with a year and a half's delayed grief reaction due to an ambivalent relationship to her late husband (second, third and fourth tasks).
3 A man with a year and a half's delayed grief reaction after two deaths separated by a short interval. Unprocessed childhood bereavement. Sparse network (second task).
4 A woman with phobic anxiety after a trauma in connection with a death.

Grief therapy for avoided grief

1 A man in crisis after parting from fiancée. Avoided grief from parents' death ten years before (second, third and fourth tasks).
2 A woman referred with lack of self-confidence and depressive traits. Avoided grief since mother's suicide when client was 13 (second, third and fourth tasks).

Grief therapy and alcohol

1 A woman referred one year after her father's death. Avoided grief reaction since mother's death when client was 14 (second task).

Grief therapy with risk of chronic grief

1 A woman referred four years after her 21-year-old daughter's sudden death. Bitterness and isolation (second, third and fourth tasks).

Crisis states

Crisis help is the first aid people need after a severe loss or trauma. This help is provided to the mourner who finds himself in a whirlwind of strong and conflicting emotions. Anyone who is still in shock needs crisis intervention so that their emotions can be released. The severe crisis in which a person is at the mercy of his emotions is of limited duration. After this, the mourner gradually becomes able to go into and out of his emotions, and the brain begins to function more normally, so that he can make plans and decisions.

Crisis help, grief help and crisis intervention

Crisis intervention and grief help after deaths of children:

Two women, Lorna and Lucy, had both lost their children in accidents. They both needed crisis intervention and grief help, because a private network cannot accommodate such dramatic losses. The help given to the two women was of differing types.

Lorna shut herself in after the accident. Her family could hear her walking about crying and screaming behind the locked door. They did not know what to do. They called a doctor, who demanded that she should open the door. In a firm voice he asked her to sit down on the sofa and breathe slowly through her mouth. He put an arm round her and said he realized that she had lost her two children. 'No greater loss can come upon anyone, Lorna, so you really need to cry. Breathe slowly and deeply so you can have a thorough cry.' He held her as if she were a child, and gradually her weeping passed into deep sobbing. He stayed sitting with her until her severe weeping had abated and she was crying quietly. In this way he had shown the family how they could help Lorna.

After this, the doctor explained to the family a bit about crisis and grief reactions. He told them about the healing there is in weeping and explained that they were welcome to join in the weeping. The family also saw that the doctor had tears in his eyes. He calmed them by saying that Lorna's violent emotions were quite normal and not a sign that she was having a nervous breakdown. The family's best help would be to accommodate her despair and be with her as long as she could not manage for herself. She could not and should not be comforted. He recommended the family to read about grief and sorrow. It has often proved useful for both the mourner and the family to read about the course of normal grief reactions, because the strong emotions may make people afraid of having a breakdown or going mad.

The doctor did not give tranquillizers. He might possibly have given a mild soporific if she had been unable to sleep for several nights and so had become unnecessarily exhausted.

Lucy, immediately after the children's deaths, was prescribed tranquillizers by her GP. For several days she had congealed into a state of shock and walked around in a drug-induced haze. A social worker referred her to us, as she regarded Lucy as seriously at risk.

Our goal was to get her out of the state of shock as quickly as possible. We asked her to cut down on the tranquillizers, but she was afraid of giving them up entirely. The first thing we did was to advise and support her to see her dead children. She was very apprehensive about doing this, so we arranged for her to take her close family with her. She managed to see the children, and so at the funeral she was able on a certain level to admit that the two little coffins contained the dead children. In this way the funeral marked the beginning of the route to a farewell.

Lucy's network was successfully mobilized. There was particularly one member of the family who had an intuitive understanding of what Lucy needed. She undertook to be responsible for co-ordinating the rest of the network in the first period after the accident.

In such a situation people cannot be alone for the first weeks. If it is not possible to make sure of a network, one will have to use hospitalization as a way of artificially ensuring that people are around the person under crisis. One of our clients was given excellent crisis help by a somatic hospital ward in the first week after a severe loss. Fortunately, this is rarely necessary.

Lorna and *Lucy* were given grief help in the group for a long time. They used it as a refuge where there were always people who could accommodate their tears. It was a great grief they had to get through, and they felt themselves that they could grieve over only one child at a time. Sometimes one child was in focus, sometimes the other. At different points they both needed help in accepting that it was proper to grieve over the children alternately. Guilt feelings arose particularly when the grief over one child was asserting itself over a long period. Did that mean that they had not loved them both equally? Here it helped that we could assure them of the normal and healthy nature of their process, and that they could see they both reacted in the same way on this point. They both used the group as a support to write farewell letters to their children when they felt ready for it. This beginning of the final farewell came six to eight months after the deaths – a beginning to a process that will take several years.

Methods

Lorna

1   Acute help to accommodate the client's emotions (second task).
2   Instruction of the network.
3   Support in grieving over one child at a time (second task).
4   Help in coping with the sense of guilt at feeling better and registering personal development (third and fourth tasks).

Lucy

1   Crisis intervention to release the first emotional reaction by giving support to see the dead children (first and second tasks).
2   Mobilizing the network.
3   As for Lorna.
4   As for Lorna.

Crisis intervention after a severely traumatic event

The life of Stephen, aged 26, had been threatened in connection with a bank robbery. He was a bank clerk and had been threatened by the bank robber so that he opened the safe. For about twenty minutes the robber had pointed a gun at Stephen before he succeeded in persuading the robber to put away the gun. The dramatic situation was terminated by the robber running away, not least as a result of Stephen's steadiness.

Right after the episode Stephen was in a kind of shock state. A couple of hours later he was overcome by an attack of weeping when he was with a couple of colleagues, who supported him well. They prevented other people from calling a doctor to give him 'something to calm him'.

In the days following Stephen was unable to sleep, and he became more and more anxious. Anxiety about the anxiety began to become a problem. Stephen asked for professional help.

Treatment

The help given to Stephen was, first, to ask him to *tell the story* down to the smallest detail and to keep him focused on the most scaring episodes. He was given the usual briefing about breathing out, breathing slowly through the mouth and relaxing. He was to imagine being face to face with the robber again and to allow himself to feel the fear he had kept away in the situation in order to stay cool. The most provocative feature was the robber's desperate eyes. We succeeded in getting Stephen to feel his fear of being shot and dying. Only by this means would he be able to let go of it. If he had repressed the fear, it would have emerged again later in attacks of anxiety and nightmares. In the longer term Stephen would have risked having regular attacks of anxiety, whose origin might with time have been forgotten.

It was explained to Stephen how he was to deal with his attacks of anxiety at home. He was particularly afraid of the sensations of being strangled. He was to use the breathing technique already used and also to focus his eyes on something outside himself. Preferably he was to look at someone else until he saw them quite clearly. He was to avoid tranquillizers and alcohol for the first period, because they lengthen the process unnecessarily. He was to make sure at first that he was not alone too much. He was to tell his friends about the experience – not just the superficial details, but also about his fear of losing his life.

Stephen followed these instructions. The episode was worked through in various ways over a total of four sessions. After that, he was able to cope with the rest, with some help from friends.

Methods

1 Crisis intervention: relax, tell the story, hold on to the most frightening details, live through the emotions. In this way the fear is annulled (second task).
2 Instruction about crisis reactions and guidelines for everyday life.
3 Share his fear of death with the network (second and third tasks).

Crisis after a death: lack of a network

Henry, aged 54, was referred three months after the death of his 85-year-old mother. His brother had died suddenly six months previously. The only remaining member of the family was a sister who was dying. She did die a fortnight later. He was closely attached to the family and had no friends. He had been divorced eight years before. Owing to various circumstances he had lost contact with his grown-up children.

He related that he sat at home rigid and in despair. He dared not begin to cry, as he was afraid that he would never stop.

Henry was in the group four times in the course of a month. He wept on the very first occasion he was in the group and enjoyed having a trainee put an arm round him. The experience in the group made him dare to cry freely at home.

When his sister died, the group supported him in going to the funeral in Jutland. On the ferry across the Great Belt he sat and wept. Here he was contacted by a couple of his own age. They had themselves lost close members of their family and were at once ready to help. This later developed into a new network with almost daily contact.

At the third group meeting we encouraged him to re-establish contact with one of the grown-up children (third task).

On the fourth occasion he came along with a farewell letter, which told of a happy reunion with one of the children and of their joint plan to re-establish contact with the others. He was still grieving over his mother and his brother and sister, but felt hope from again being able to have contact with his grown-up children.

Methods

1   The group acted as a temporary network, which could cope with his emotions and give support to his actions (the funeral) (second and third tasks).
2   Support to re-establish a network (third task).

Delayed grief

People with delayed grief have normally solved the first task, that of recognizing the loss, but they have not gone on to release the emotions.

In a number of cases it may be necessary to postpone the emotional reaction, if there are many important tasks to be done in connection with the death. There may be business to be carried on, or a show that cannot be cancelled. But the practical tasks must not be allowed to take up so much room that the grief is constantly postponed. If that occurs, the person may come to pay a price for it in the form of a reduced quality of life and symptoms of anxiety, depression, intense guilt feelings, somatic illness, suicidal thoughts and so on.

Behind all pathological grief reactions lies the fear of separation. A pathological grief reaction is a sign that the person cannot cope with the separation without help. If the emotional reaction is still absent after more than a few weeks, we must regard the grief as being delayed and offer help.

Unfortunately, those around often overlook the danger signals. 'She seems a bit depressed, and she is often ill, but that's hardly surprising, when she has lost her son/husband/mother. She doesn't feel she has anything to live for any more.' This attitude means that someone in delayed grief is often left in the lurch.

When a client is referred to us, we therefore always want to know how the grief reaction has proceeded hitherto. It is characteristic that the mourner tries to make life go on as if nothing had happened. There may be gloominess and anxiety, or an artificial gaiety and restless activity. Often there are many guilt feelings, as with Sandra (see Chapter Two), who had run away from her mother's death-bed. An increase of alcohol consumption or anxiolytic drugs may contribute to keeping the emotions at bay. The grave is seldom visited – and mostly out of a sense of duty. Sometimes the deceased's ashes have been buried anonymously, so there is no place to visit. Often we find that the client has wept little or not at all at the funeral and that they have hardly wept since.

Just as the line between normal and pathological grief is a blurred one, so too is that between delayed and avoided grief. But the main rule is that in delayed grief the emotions are more accessible than with avoided grief. The first year after the death we would therefore call a grief delayed because the emotions may be presumed to be fairly accessible. But this is not always the case, as the next example shows. We were hard put to it to penetrate to Tina's emotions.

So it is the accessibility of the emotions that decides whether a grief is to be called delayed or avoided. As will appear, the treatment methods are more or less the same in both cases.

Grief therapy in delayed grief

Grief therapy in grief delayed for six months. Traumatic illness. Untimely death. Dependency.

Tina, aged 32, was referred to us because of frequent attacks of anxiety and a feeling of unreality and emptiness. She was in perpetual hectic activity and was smiling almost all the time. She had no emotional surplus available for her 3-year-old daughter, Charlotte. Six months previously she had lost her husband Peter after a long and stressful illness. She had been very closely attached to Peter, who was ten years older.

As a child she had been over-protected by two loving parents who were unable to lay down limits for her. She describes herself as lively, rather lazy, and dominating in her adolescence and youth. She found in Peter a loving husband, who treated her rather paternally and caringly and did not make many demands upon her. So her relationship with Peter was a repeat of her childhood pattern. When Charlotte was born it was largely Peter who looked after her. She was 'Daddy's girl'.

Peter became seriously ill with cancer and the roles were exchanged. For long periods Tina looked after her husband at home, while he shrank to being skin and bones. Gradually she lost contact with him because of the large doses of painkillers. But Peter protected Tina to the last. He knew himself that he was going to die, but he did not talk about it to Tina. All the time she preserved the hope that he would survive.

Treatment

At the first group meeting, Tina merely said that she had to work on Peter's death. On the second occasion we started on the traumatic course of his illness. We got her to tell about the 'hardest' periods during his illness and about her fear that Peter would die. She had not previously dared to formulate this fear to herself even, and certainly not to other people.

We used our intense compassion and authority to penetrate to Tina's blocked emotions. But Tina's defence mechanisms were strong, and among other things she used her recurrent smile to keep her emotions at bay. 'I was indeed ready to drop it all when I had been here a couple of times, simply because I felt it was too hard. You got me to go on, and today I am very glad. I have found quite an incredible ballast here,' she wrote in her farewell letter to the group.

She was given the homework assignment of writing a detailed letter to Peter about the time of his illness and her fear of the disease. At the next group meeting we got her to read it out slowly with his picture lying in front of her, and we followed the same procedure as with Sandra (see pages 39–47). At last we got her to be very serious while the whole letter was read aloud. But although she repeated the most stressful sections, we did not get her to enter into her emotions.

Her next task was to visit the grave. But this did not elicit her emotions either. She again complained of the fear, emptiness, tiredness and the sensation of living in a bell-jar. She had difficulty in sleeping and mentioned that she had to drink wine to make her fall asleep. When she mentioned alcohol, we pricked up our ears. She herself was quite surprised to discover that she had developed a fixed pattern of uncorking a bottle of wine every afternoon after work and emptying it before bedtime. She felt she needed the wine if she was going to have the calmness to be with Charlotte and to get to sleep. In the group she discovered that the price of this 'calmness' was that she had come to a halt in her grief work. She was caught up in a negative, self-reinforcing spiral in which her fear would gradually grow greater and greater because of the avoided emotions. So her need to numb herself with alcohol would also increase.

After this, Tina made a contract with the group not to touch alcohol or tranquillizers for a month. The change proved not to be nearly as hard as she had feared. She told her friends about her decision and was fairly well backed up. When the alcohol was out of the picture, the turning-point in the process arrived. In her next letter to Peter, she took up her great sense of loss and feeling of impotence at having been left with responsibility for the child who had so much been his. At the reading of this letter, our sympathetic comments finally made Tina let go, and she began to weep deeply. We were relieved that she had finally got started on the second task. 'Nini's and Marianne's often tough questions finally got me going, and Lise from the group kept me at the tasks I undertook. Thanks for your tireless belief that we all can, if we dare and wish to.'

In the following period, Tina obviously felt 'worse'. It seemed as if she had woken up from an anaesthetic and was now beginning to feel that bereavement and despair. At first she could weep only in the group. It was some time before she felt sufficiently secure with her friends to dare to let the tears flow freely in their company.

It was a difficult time. When the sense of loss overwhelmed her, it might sometimes feel bottomless. At the same time she noticed how the anxiety and the bell-jar sensations disappeared in step with her daring to feel both the pain and the anger, which came along later. Gradually she became able to go into and out of her grief. When she had wept in the morning, she could go to work in a soft mood and concentrate reasonably on her work assignments. Perhaps in the course of the day something would happen to remind her of Peter. Then the tears came back. Gradually she learned that an attack of weeping that was shared with a colleague who was her confidante never lasted longer then ten to fifteen minutes. This made her less afraid of going into her emotions. Later she was able, for moments, for half or whole hours, to be in good spirits. When she went to bed in the evening, she might perhaps find herself weeping again with loneliness.

Gradually it dawned upon her how much she had lost because Peter and she had not managed to talk about his death and to say goodbye. Peter had protected her to the last. 'Peter knew he was going to die, but he tried in every way to conceal it from me. I let him do it – not aware of what was really involved. This repression has given guilt feelings at not having picked up the little signals that Peter was actually sending out.'

Tina was given the task of talking to Peter's closest friend, with whom Peter had shared his fear of death. Why had Peter not confided in Tina in this way? What did the friend know about it? It was important for Tina's process that she should be able to piece together as clear a picture as possible of the true situation. The chat with the friend would at the same time be a task of sharing her thoughts and feelings with someone other than the group and her colleague at work (third task).

After her conversation with the friend she became angry for the first time that Peter, with his over-protectiveness, had cheated her out of his confidence. 'I have been given help to feel, besides the guilt, also anger that Peter could not bloody well share his fear with me.'

With her letter to Peter Tina took a decisive step. She now regarded herself as being an adult and the equal of her husband who had always had a protective role towards her. In this way she gained a strength and independence which she needed for going on living.

Later she entered a fresh period of despair at being left alone with the child for whom Peter had borne the main responsibility, and anger at his dying and leaving her so shortly after bringing a child into the world. Afterwards, she again found new strength, and her relationship to the child changed. She gradually accepted the role of a single parent and felt joy at her close contact with Charlotte. Mother and daughter began to talk about Peter together and look at pictures of him. Now and again Charlotte saw her mother crying, and was told it was because she was missing Daddy. In this way Tina also allowed her daughter to grieve. At the nursery school they noticed that Charlotte had calmed down after Tina had become more open about their shared bereavement. Charlotte began to talk more about her father.

During the latter part of her time with the group, Tina was given support to dare sometimes to hand Charlotte over to other members of the family and friends so that she could get a bit of her own life. The child's anxiety at being away from her mother was naturally increased after her father's death, and she protested when her mother wanted to leave her. All the same, the group deemed that, with her present good development nine months after the father's death, Charlotte would benefit more from experiencing a brief separation from her mother under secure circumstances than continuing to cling to her. After all, Charlotte experienced separation from her mother every day at nursery school and got daily confirmation that her mother always came back to fetch her. Charlotte cried the first time Tina went, but she soon calmed down with her grandma.

This task was also an element in getting Tina to use her friends in a new way (third task). Hitherto, she had only shown her grief to her colleague and to Peter's friend. Now she was to visit friends and tell them about her thoughts and painful feelings about being alone.

Tina was a member of the group for eight months, but the intensive work lasted only about three months, after which the group became a place where she found support for the third and fourth tasks. Like many others, in the first month Tina attended twice a week, and then once a week, until after a good three months she only came every fortnight. After four months she came only occasionally. 'Although I have not made use of you in recent months by being physically present in the group, I have been aware all the time of the safety net you are. In a way I have been making use of even more of the experience we have together given each other.'

After eight months she felt ready to round off the course by coming several times running to chat about how she was getting on with her new life. Then she wrote her farewell letter to Peter, which was read aloud to the group with a good many tears. The following week came her farewell letter to the group. This letter, passages of which have already been quoted, concludes:

I find it hard to find words for what you who have cried with me have meant . . . but I have again the faith that together we can handle life, even though the grief at losing Peter is today in many ways stronger than when I started in the autumn. Finally I must tell you that I once believed that I could cope with just anything at all on my own, and you have helped me to understand and feel that only together are we strong. Many thanks to you all.

Tina writes that she once believed that she was able to cope with absolutely anything on her own. This 'alone but strong' attitude had made her so vulnerable that she had to find a man ten years older to protect her. Peter's death and her course of attendance in the group helped her to settle accounts with her double role as the dominant/helpless one and to find a role in between, so that she could both receive help from others and be a responsible mother for Charlotte. Thus Tina became more flexible about her optimum distance to other people.

Around the time Tina finished with the group, we had four young widows with little children. We called on them to form a self-help group, and this succeeded for a period in spite of considerable geographical distance between them.

Methods

1 Four attempts to release the emotions: (a) 'tell the story', (b) write a letter about the 'story', (c) read the letter aloud to the group, (d) visit the cemetery (second task).
2 Contract on giving up alcohol and drugs for a month.
3 New letter to husband and reading it aloud (second task).
4 Arrangement about who she would cry with (second and third tasks).

5 Conversation with husband's friend to get the facts about husband's final illness and to practise sharing her feelings with others (second and third tasks).
6 Work on anger with husband (second task).
7 Support in weeping with her child and talking to her about her father (second and third tasks).
8 Contract about visiting a friend while the child was looked after (third task).
9 Farewell letter to husband (fourth task).
10 Farewell letter to the group, taking stock of the course of treatment.

Grief therapy with grief delayed a year and a half after a traumatic illness; untimely death; much delayed anger

Thirty-nine-year-old Kirsten's husband (also 39) died suddenly after six years' severe physical illness. The illness had gradually changed him from being a lively, active man, who looked after her, the children, and helped with the housework, into an increasingly alcoholized, helpless and demanding husband. He envied Kirsten her healthy life and tried to isolate her from the outside world. When he died, she was at first shocked, and later she was tortured by her angry thoughts against him. Whenever she stood by his grave, she felt like kicking his gravestone. She felt guilt at these thoughts and feelings, but they did not go away. The children cried and missed their father, and she felt she ought to be able to share their grief, but she could not. She was rather irritated at them. She felt that a wall was growing up between her and the children.

Treatment

She joined the group a year and a half after her husband's death. At first she was given support in accepting that she felt angry and cheated that her husband had become so changed and had dominated her life in such a stressful way. She wrote angry letters to her dead husband and thereby got rid of some of the feelings of guilt over her anger. She had been much ashamed at her husband's alcoholism and had concealed it as much as possible while he was alive.

To cultivate her network, she chose to share the hard feelings and the humiliating experiences with two friends who had seen little but her brave smile during all the husband's illness. With this she was also getting going on the third task.

117

The turning-point in the therapy came when Kirsten, affected by another client, began to cry about the great relief she had felt when her husband died. After this we took every opportunity to give her openings for feeling the relief again. We had her tell all new group members that she was grieving over the loss of her husband and that the hardest thing was that she was relieved that he was dead. At first she said this with many tears and guilt feelings. Gradually she was able to say it more calmly. Little by little, positive memories began to emerge of her life with her husband before he fell ill, and there was room for grief that she had lost the husband she had once loved and who was the father of her children. She had lost him when he became ill. When she had felt both the anger and the loss, the way was paved for the final farewell. She could now share her grief with her children, and in this way contact with them was improved.

Methods

1 Give the client leave to feel anger and encourage her to express it in letters to her spouse (second task).
2 Break the secrecy about the alcoholism and so on with friends (third task).
3 Turning-point when we support the 'forbidden' feeling of relief which another client's work triggers off (second task).
4 Many repetitions that it is permissible to feel the relief (second task).
5 Support her in feeling the loss of her husband as he was before he became ill (second task).
6 Suggest she shares her sense of loss with the children (second and third tasks).

Grief therapy with grief delayed a year and a half; two losses in a fortnight; sparse network; unprocessed loss in childhood

Sidney, aged 55, was referred to the grief group with a delayed grief reaction a year and a half after his wife and sister had died with a fortnight's interval between the deaths. He had scarcely wept at all in connection with the deaths. His own doctor had given him a sedative for a while, but he had himself tapered off the use to nothing. He was living an empty and dreary life, did his job and had contact only with his grown-up children.

One day, to his own amazement, he began to sob aloud in the middle of a shopping centre. He applied to the local welfare office and was given good crisis help. However, the social worker thought he needed more support and referred him to us. At her suggestion he had laid the foundations of a new network by contacting various neighbours and sharing his grief with them.

At the preliminary interview he told how he was troubled with guilt feelings about having been away from the sick-room when his wife died. This had clearly prevented him saying his final farewell to her.

The routine questions about his childhood revealed that his father had left home suddenly when Sidney was 12. For some years there was sporadic contact, after which his father completely disappeared. As an adult he had sought out his father, but the irascible, self-absorbed man had had nothing to give his son.

But Sidney had never been able to abandon hope of sometime obtaining his father's acceptance and love. Even as a 55-year-old he thought almost daily with longing about his father, who was still alive. He regularly had to talk himself out of contacting his father, with inevitable disappointment to follow. Once or twice a year he had given way to the longing and visited his father. The unsuccessful visit had then curbed the urge for contact for another six to twelve months. Sidney had thus much mental energy invested in the longing for him. His delayed grief reaction was thus not only founded on a lack of network, but also in the unprocessed grief at being abandoned by his father as a 12-year-old. It was striking that at the preliminary interview Sidney had tears in his eyes when mentioning his wife and sister, but he wept properly when he spoke of his father's desertion.

Treatment

Sidney wrote three letters in the group. The first was a farewell letter to his wife, in which he managed to speak of his feeling of guilt. The second was an angry letter to his father about his desertion and Sidney's longing for him through all those years. 'Why did you leave me alone with the pain, when you knew that I had just lost my two dear girls; you didn't come to the funeral but sent a bunch of flowers instead. I sat there in church with the card from the flowers, weeping because you wouldn't come, but perhaps you were much too proud to come? I thought: if only you had come, then we could have had a real chat together, but it is only wishful thinking on my part.' Here Sidney shows clearly how the disappointment and anger with his father entered into and disturbed the grief concerning his wife and sister. The tears in the church came to be concerned with the childhood loss instead of the present losses.

Finally Sidney wrote a farewell letter to his father. By this time the good memories of the time before his father left the family were emerging and, keeping hold of them, Sidney was able to give up the hope of ever getting his childhood's emotional needs met.

Sidney came to the group once a week for seven weeks. Besides the letters, which were to be the most important part of his therapy, he used the group as a network for his grief. This training in using other people in a qualitatively better manner had great influence on his way of using his network.

Methods

1 Re-telling the events around his wife's and sister's deaths (the second task).
2 Farewell letter to his wife (the fourth task).
3 Two letters to the father who left him when he was 12: the first about anger and disappointment; the second a farewell letter to the hope of receiving his acceptance and love (the fourth task).
4 Practice in using a network (the third task).

Extinction of anxiety after a trauma related to a death

Andrea, aged 50, lost her husband of many years after a lengthy illness. She had looked after him at home during the last period, and Owen passed peacefully away holding Andrea's hand. Andrea kept vigil by the body for the whole night. 'It was as if he was asleep,' she said.

The next day she asked the undertaker to place the body in a coffin in the living room. When she saw Owen in the coffin, she suddenly realized that she would never see him any more. She felt deeply shocked.

Six months later she was still bothered by the sight of Owen in the coffin. It would come many times during the day, and she was unhappy that she could not remember Owen as he was before he died. She avoided the living room and became more and more anxious about the unpleasant sight.

So our form of treatment at first was to help Andrea with the trauma: the sight of her husband's coffin in the living room. It was impossible to assess how much she was at risk of a pathological development until she had got control of the anxiety which had developed into a phobia about the living room.

Treatment

When Andrea had attended the group a few times and felt reasonably secure, we suggested she should work on her phobia. Although it scared her a bit, she very much wanted to be rid of the sight of her husband in his coffin, so that she could once more use the largest room in the flat.

We got her settled comfortably, gave her briefing about relaxing her body and about calm and slow breathing. After that, she related several times how her husband had looked that morning before the undertaker came, how he looked when he was laid in the coffin, and what it was like to look at him lying in the coffin. When she had recounted it a couple of times, we asked her to relate in detail how he looked in the coffin, what clothes he was wearing, what his hair, his skin and so on looked like. Finally we asked her to imagine the lid being laid on the coffin. Andrea was very anxious during the whole proceeding, but she left the group without anxiety.

The tasks she was given on the next two occasions were first to tell about the sight in detail to a friend and then to sit in the living room with the friend and again tell about the sight, while she herself saw it before her in the room.

After this, the intensity of the vision waned, and in time it disappeared. She had to have support to use the living room for some hours every day, and after some weeks she was able to use the room without any anxiety.

Methods

Here we used a method of behaviour therapy: extinction. The client had developed an anxiety about the anxiety. She was afraid of the fear that would arise if she went into the room. The purpose of the method is to get the client into the fear-filled situation long enough for her to discover that it is not dangerous, after which the fear dies away.

The phases of the method are:

1 Re-living the situation in the imagination, by which the anxiety is processed.
2 Re-telling the same situation to a friend, perhaps with some anxiety.
3 Re-telling the situation at the anxiety-evoking place.
4 Support to be in the living room some hours every day, until the recurrent anxiety had waned.

If these methods had proved inadequate, we would have asked the client to draw the situation and show it to the group. We might also have got her to describe the situation in a letter to her husband.

Avoided grief

Avoided grief differs from delayed grief in that the feelings are hidden further away. Many years may have passed since the bereavement, and the symptoms about which the client complains rarely lead the therapist directly back to the grief. It requires insight to see behind the psychosomatic and mental symptoms to identify the loss which triggered them off.

In the introduction to the chapter about the four tasks, avoided grief is thoroughly described (pages 27–8), and in the conclusion of the chapter about risk groups and deciding treatment we amplify how to identify avoided grief with a view to undertaking grief therapy (pages 82–3).

In this chapter we want to give an impression of work on avoided grief. The examples all come from our work with grief groups, in which the intense emotional atmosphere is a great help in reaching the avoided emotions. But it will also be possible to use the methods in individual treatment. As an introduction to this section, we want to print a farewell letter from a woman of 46.

> She was referred to us from a welfare office, where she was being recommended for a pension on account of dementia. A shrewd caseworker referred her to us, as she discovered that the client had not worked through the cot death of her baby, which had taken place ten years before. Excerpts from her farewell letter to the baby are included in the section on the fourth task (page 62). The farewell letter to the group gives the essence of the intensely painful but life-giving process which the work on an avoided grief was to the client.

> Dear Nini, Marianne, and you whom I have contacted through coming here.
> My farewell to you hurts a bit, but at the same time I know the time has come. I started in August after an interview with you and my caseworker Elsebeth. At that time I was so far gone that it was with the greatest difficulty I could be faced with someone strange to me without an almost panic confusion. You asked me whether I had the *courage* to join in your group. My little baby of 8 months had died, ten years before. I was tested, showing a greater memory loss than usual for my age, and I did not myself straight away make a connection with Carol's name, nor did I ever mention it. You said, 'Have you got the *courage*?' If I had been myself, I would probably have backed off and said, 'Have you?' Where others have given up, you dared to start. So it was with rather mixed feelings I began with you. To my own amazement, I settled

in, began to open up and concentrate, and I grasped a little. There was progress, so my memory came back slowly, and what I did not know, you did. Like lightning I went on one downturn worse than the next; my grief at my little daughter became today's grief, I wept and by your side I was given all the support which I should never have 'survived' without. I had merely been existing, on a dream of that time. Through you I have learnt that many a time the answer lies in ourselves. Going through the letter to Carol, it was not anger, but a grief at ten wasted years of my life. I heard a sentence here, it went, 'anyone who ventures loses his footing for a while, but anyone who ventures nothing loses himself'. How true that is. I did not venture my grief and lost myself. You helped me to dare, there are not words enough for my gratitude, for what you have done not just for me but also the participants in the group. We all know how much of yourselves you give to be able to carry through your knowledge to positive results. I myself know that it became a change into a life which each day approaches my own ego.

Grief therapy for avoided grief at parents' death twelve years before; present grief over fiancée

Robert, aged 26, came to us in a state of panic because his fiancée of a year was threatening to break off their relationship. He knew from experience that it was very hard for him to end relationships. He remembered how once, for two years after breaking with a girl, he had sought her out again and again and subjected himself to many humiliations, but just could not keep away. He had wept a lot over the loss of his former girlfriend. Even when after two years he accepted that there was no hope of carrying on the relationship, he went on missing her. He was reluctant to go through an ordeal like that again.

We had to go back to his childhood to understand the background to this profound dependency upon girlfriends and inability to accept and live through a breach. He had grown up in a home with a self-sacrificing mother and a withdrawn, bitter father, who was a partial invalid after a road accident. His sister, six years older, moved away from home when he was 14. Shortly afterwards, his mother suddenly died of a heart attack. Robert did not react by grieving at his mother's death, but by supporting his withdrawn father. Before his mother's death, he was passing through adolescent rebellion against his father, but this was now partially stopped, as it had become more difficult to allow the angry feelings to find expression, because his father was grieving over his mother's death.

Just under a year later, Robert, now 15, found his father dead; he had committed suicide. Not even in this situation did Robert react emotionally, but just sat down and had breakfast.

Nor did any grief reaction to his father's death come later. When his mother died, Robert had found a method of keeping his grief at bay, and so his far more ambivalent emotions towards his father were also avoided. After his parents' death there followed some difficult years, when he was put in a foster home and a hostel. He always kept his emotions at a distance by being slightly depressive, sleeping a lot, and busying himself with mechanics, radios and so on. If he stopped being busy, he got a headache and needed more sleep. He had hidden away all the pictures of his parents and avoided the street in which he had lived as a child.

His parents' early deaths had given him a rootless feeling, and when he began to have girlfriends, this gave him an experience of again belonging to someone. But his self-confidence was very slight so he hardly dared to express his own needs if they differed from his girlfriend's, for fear of losing her. Robert became such a 'soft' man that he was a bore to be with.

Robert is relatively typical of a number of our young clients with avoided childhood grief. Of course the details of their life stories differ, but common to all is their difficulty in coping with a couple relationship. Some give up more or less in advance and isolate themselves. Others have many changing partners. Yet others like Robert become conflict-shunning and much too dependent.

We have good experience of working through the losses of childhood down to the ages of 9 to 10 years. In a few cases we have tried to help clients whose losses have lain even farther back, but have had to give up. The clients could not feel the grief in the same way, perhaps because it was too hard to make out what they remembered for themselves and what they had been told about the dead father or mother. In other words, the pictures were too indistinct.

Treatment

Robert attended the group eighteen times over a period of four months. His fiancée Kirsten had broken with him finally shortly after he had started in the group. The many emotions this entailed and the intense emotional mood of the group made it relatively easy for Robert to return to the loss of his mother and father. Not all clients with avoided grief are so 'lucky' as to have an acute loss when they start in the group. In that case, there is need for some 'thawing out' before they can find their way back to their avoided grief.

Robert's first assignment in the group was to say goodbye to Kirsten. He used letter-writing to keep hold of all his own contradictory feelings. Robert was given the group's support in sorting out what concerned Kirsten and what was bound up with the yearning for the home he had lost so early in life.

For the first time he became able to set limits on Kirsten and ask her to fetch her own furniture from his flat, instead of being the perpetually willing partner.

In his farewell letter to the group he wrote:

Helped along by you two, I have managed to say goodbye to my father, my mother, and two ex-girlfriends. And it was high time. The support I was given when Kirsten vamoosed has also been incredibly important to me. Of the four farewell letters I wrote, the one to my father was the most important. The first time I chatted to you, one of the things you said was that the father I had been fond of when I was little was somewhere inside me. And that turned out to be quite right.

Robert's letter to his father was written in several bouts. The first contained anger at his father's tyranny in the home during his many years as an invalid. Then followed the letter to his mother, which was filled with love and gratitude for her contribution to the home, but it also contained new angles like criticism of his mother's over-indulgence of the father's role as an invalid.

After his mother had come off her pedestal, Robert was able to settle accounts with his role as the one who always had to support women. This cleared the way for the return of memories of an inventive father who played amusing games with his son before the road accident. In his second letter to his father he was able to express his pleasure at these memories. This became crucial for Robert's growing respect for himself as a man.

Hearing other people honestly telling about their thoughts and feelings has had great importance for me. I have particularly been glad to hear that women can love men and miss them. That has meant that today I feel worth much more as a man .... I have become much wiser. I feel I know myself better and that I know other people better. And whereas I used to believe I was so different from other people, I now discover that there isn't all that difference when you come down to it, i.e. when the masks are off. How nice it is to talk with people when they are being themselves.

As this shows, being together with the others both in and after the group meeting was of importance to Robert, because here he was getting contact of a quality he had never before experienced. We supported him in avoiding a fresh girlfriend relationship for the time being, advice which to our relief he followed. We were fairly certain it would not be easy, because while he was in the group he changed from being a good-looking boy into an attractive young man.

His farewell letter to the group ended: 'You have been gentle and tough as the situation required.... I used to feel I was weak, now I feel very strong.'

Method adopted

1 The group's atmosphere and intensity eased the opening to the avoided emotions (second task).
2 Being with the group gave practice in using a network (third task).
3 Support in trying out new behaviour towards ex-fiancée (third task).
4 Four letters (second and third tasks).
5 Farewell letter to the group taking stock of the course of therapy (third and fourth tasks).

Grief therapy for avoided grief after mother's suicide when the client was 13

Pamela, aged 23, applied to the Student Counselling Service because of great problems in choosing a course of study. She was intelligent, had succeeded in school examinations, and would be able to take up many courses of study. She had investigated all the possibilities very thoroughly, but all options seemed equally uninteresting to her. She made a dreary impression and complained of experiencing life through a bell-jar. She did not want help with any other problems than her choice of study. On being questioned further, it turned out that her mother had committed suicide when Pamela was 13. She hardly remembered her mother. After her death all mementoes of her had been removed, and she was not spoken about. Pamela had not seen her mother dead and had not been at the funeral.

Our assessment was that Pamela was living in her bell-jar with an avoided grief that was ten years old. It was not surprising that with so little contact with her emotions (her true self) she was unable to sense which study course would be the right one for her. So we decided to offer her a place in the grief group.

It was not easy to get her motivated. With the best will in the world she could not see the connection between her mother dying ten years before and her being unable now to decide what to study! But she did agree to attend the grief group a few times to have a look.

Treatment

For the first month she did not say much in the group. She was asked each time how she felt. Often she answered that she felt out of place, but she always agreed to come the next time. Gradually we could see that she was becoming more and more involved in what was going on with the others. In other words, she was being 'softened up' emotionally. Cracks were appearing in the bell-jar.

When she finally felt ready to work on her mother's death, there was the problem that she could hardly remember her. So a considerable part of her therapy consisted in making her mother 'live' before she could bid farewell to her.

She was given a series of tasks: visiting her father, grandmother and other kin who had known her mother, and gathering photographs and stories about who her mother was and the circumstances of her death. She became very absorbed in this work and changed her attitude to some of these network persons during the course of it.

The emotional breakthrough came when she was with a girlfriend and her good, warm mother. Here she could suddenly sense what she had missed out on. Her own mother's long-term mental problems which had culminated in suicide had meant that there had never been much surplus for Pamela. For the first time she began to cry. After that, there followed painful grief work over a childhood without a caring mother. She wrote her way through much of it in diary entries, letters and poems.

Her choice of study was mentioned on one of the last occasions she was in the group. She now knew what she wanted to study and had become absorbed in it. We were never consulted. When, through her grief work, she had made contact with parts of her true self, she was able to find out what she wanted.

Her farewell letter to the group describes how she experienced the grief therapy:

Dear Crazy Group,
 I am not very literary and so I rarely read, but I have picked up one quote from literature. It is by Blicher:
 'The greatest grief this world allows
 is losing someone who is dear.'
It has taken me ten years to understand how much grief, pain, fear and anger has been bound up with losing my mother, who committed suicide when I was 13.

During this period, when for the first time I have seriously got to grips with the greatest grief in my life, some things are the same and yet not the same. I'll explain:

I felt odd when I started here, I felt peculiar during the course, and I feel strange now.

I can recall the sensation of total chaos when I attended the Student Counselling for the first time, and I clearly remember how the sensation was turned into pent-up snorting rage when I was cunningly enticed into working in this group, which centres on pain and bereavement. That was not my problem, I felt, and it has taken time to realize what incredibly strong emotions lay bound up in the past, which I had hidden away in order to survive.

The work here has been hard but necessary. It has been hard to face up to it that a lot of pain lies behind it, that there has been too much madness, too many years' loneliness, and one suicide too many in my background, and that has for good or ill shaped me, given me some scars in my soul, but not gutted it. It has also been hard to show strong emotions in a large company, and it is still hard; but it has become a bit easier, and it is nice to be able to cry now and again, and particularly to get really cross, and also to dare to show the zest and positive madness that has always been inside me.

For a Mick Jagger lives inside us all who feels like screaming, kicking, laughing your arse off, shocking the family, wriggling your hips and being as daft as possible.

For me, being in the group has been hard, but invaluable, and I hardly dare to think what might have happened if I had not come here. I feel it's like having been handed a will in which piece by piece, I have gone through the different things that were on offer and then have made a careful assessment of what I want to inherit and take with me into life. I know that I do not want to inherit my mother's illness, her fear and pain and all it has brought, and I shall go on fighting for that. I feel that here I have been given excellent help to find my roots and thus myself.

Well, it is still a rather confused snake who is creeping out of the group after getting through a difficult passage in the desert. It is now sloughing off its skin, and it hurts, but it is necessary, for it has got to match up to the new times coming.

Thanks to you all in the group and to the constructive part of me which made this possible. I'll miss you a lot, but I can manage all right without you today.

Kindest regards from Pamela.

Methods adopted

1 Patience and rock-like faith that the healthy grief reaction would get started. Agreements from one session to the next to come back again.
2 The group's emotional intensity (first and second tasks).
3 The group gatherings after the sessions (third task).
4 Conversations with network persons about her mother's life and the circumstances of her suicide (first, second and third tasks).
5 Obtaining photos and showing them in the group (second task).
6 Support in using friends' mothers (second and third tasks).
7 Letters, diary entries, poems.
8 Farewell letter to the group.

Grief therapy with avoided and delayed grief complicated by many years of alcohol abuse

Lene, aged 36, is an example of a client whom grief therapy did not succeed in helping. She was referred by a welfare office a year after her father's death. She had only cried a little, although she had been very closely attached to him. Her mother had died unexpectedly when Lene was 14. She had learnt from her family that one ought not to show one's feelings. Thus her father never spoke of her mother after she had died. Lene avoided the grief.

Her adolescence was marked by a good deal of other insecurity, and for periods she was boarded out with members of the family. As an adult she lived for some years in a stressful marriage that ended in divorce. After that, she attached herself closely to her father, whom she visited every weekend and was often on the telephone with. Her symptoms were lack of self-assurance, achievement anxiety, depression and periods of alcohol abuse. She had considerable fear of other people, which often meant that she stayed away from work.

She had had all these symptoms for many years, but they had become worse after her father's death. Her network consisted of three friends who were willing to support and listen. She was not abusing alcohol at the time she was referred to us, and she had not done so for the three months previously. She had shown earlier that she could take Antabuse during periods when the urge for alcohol was too strong.

She cried a good deal at the preliminary interview, but also said that she did not like talking about her father's death and that she was ashamed at crying with other people. But she did seem minded to accept help.

Before we agreed to try grief therapy, we considered a number of factors. Alcohol abuse always has the aim of numbing emotions. We had to assume that one of the reasons was to keep at bay the avoided grief over her mother. As Lene had been unable to process this grief, she had also had to keep at a distance her grief over her divorce and her father's death. Otherwise, the one grief would have drawn the other along with it, and with her fear of emotions she would not have been able to cope with this on her own. Would she be able to manage it with the support of the grief group? Would the group's mixture of intensity and security help her to the turning-point where she would learn to accommodate her emotions – primarily, the delayed grief over her father? Would she be able to get over her shame at weeping among other people and learn to make better use of her network? Would she, through her grief over her parents, emerge from her great longing for security and take greater responsibility for her own life?

Our greatest misgiving was the alcohol abuse. If this had arisen in connection with the most recent death, as had been the case with Tina, this would have been no obstacle. But for many years the alcohol had been 'protecting' Lene from unpleasant emotions. Would she be able to cope without resorting to this escape route when she began to feel the pain of her losses?

Her great wish for a change made us offer her help despite her alcohol abuse. We prepared her for an increase in her desire for alcohol at the start. We made a bargain with her to tell us if the urge became strong or if she started drinking again.

Treatment

As we had foreseen, the group was a strong experience, but Lene was proud of having coped with it and of having cried a little in the group. Nevertheless, she stayed away after the first two times for three weeks, possibly because we had asked her at too early a stage to begin a letter to her father.

In response to our urging by telephone, she came again a few times, but then stayed away again and, in spite of all urgings, she did not come any more. She said that she felt 'too insecure' in the group.

This unsuccessful grief therapy illustrates the problems we have run into when we have been working with clients with long-term abuse of alcohol. These clients have learnt at home that emotions are 'dangerous'. Lene's father demonstrated this attitude by never mentioning her mother after she had died. Many have also seen their parents using alcohol for this purpose..

In grief therapy, the clients have to learn the opposite. They have to learn to endure the necessary healing pain. It is no easy task when in alcohol they have a 'friend' that can always make the pain go away again.

Our experience with alcoholics is not very extensive, and we have only succeeded in helping a few. We have come to the view that alcoholics ought to undergo a deep therapy focusing on their alcohol abuse before they come to grief therapy.

Our poor experience with alcoholics has meant that we have never attempted grief therapy with real abusers of drugs. But we have been able to help many people who have had a regular consumption of anxiolytics and alcohol *in connection with losses* which had taken place within the previous couple of years.

One client who gradually managed to accommodate the pain without alcohol was a 22-year-old woman who had used alcohol as a solace since she was 13. In the group she was working on her grief at having to say goodbye to a man friend who had given her much security since she was 15. As part of her therapeutic work she decided to say goodbye to the alcohol. We print her farewell letter to alcohol, because we think that it illustrates the grief work which any alcoholic has to go through when they are to say goodbye to a 'friend' who has never failed them in the short term.

Dear Alcohol,

Now your turn has come, now your bad influence is going to get out of my life. I want to cope with the difficult and hard situations without you. It will be hard, but to my amazement I have survived a whole month without the chance of a single beer, despite several times being in situations where I traditionally get drunk, to get away from it all, because I cannot or dare not cope with the feelings that come up inside me. They are feelings like desertedness, loneliness, unwantedness, deep grief and frustration. I have been the victim of these feelings, and yet I didn't drink. I did not believe I would survive it, and at the same time I felt it to be ridiculous that I, a grown woman, could stand there and quite seriously weigh up whether I should go out and rinse my mouth in a cup of beer, for it would have a taste of the real stuff, and perhaps I should get just a little of the old assurance? I have noticed how my body was trembling inside, my hands began to sweat and the panic rose up inside me because I could not give way, just a little bit, to my desire for you. It has also made me afraid of the power you have over me, and at the same time I have felt a great assurance when I have taken my Dipsan, for then I have something/someone to share the responsibility, the burden, with.

For it is a heavy responsibility to take. I do feel a bit that I am letting down an old friend of many years. A friend who has never deserted me or failed me when I needed him. When everybody else has left me, you have always been there, I have always been able to lean on you, console myself with you and share my sorrows with you. But I don't want you, all the same, for the price of getting you is too great, you demand too much of me. There are no compromises for you and me, it is over, past, done with for ever.

Goodbye, cool taste of lager, goodbye the inner calm you gave me, even though it was false, goodbye to the friends you gave me, to the life-style you required of me, goodbye to the wretched life you offered me, goodbye to dependence on you, goodbye to the trembles, goodbye early mornings when I have not dared to get out of bed without five of you and your kind, goodbye you rotten surrogate for a father, a mother, and a home to belong to.'

Chronic grief

When someone in chronic grief tells about their loss, one's heart often goes out to them. The wound seems so open and raw that one imagines that the death has occurred within recent months or at most a year or so. Great is one's surprise to hear that the bereavement is four, eight or even ten years old.

The immediate impression is that chronic mourners cannot cope with their lives without the deceased. Without the dead they can see no meaning in their lives. As a rule they isolate themselves and do not take up the challenges that are necessary for having a life with even a little content. Their thoughts and feelings centre upon the death, and they often feel unfairly treated and bitter that the world around does not seem to appreciate the extent of their loss, but rather attempts to encourage them to get going on new activities.

In chronic grief the relationship between the mourner and the dead person was very close. Often they have 'lived for each other'. Two parents in chronic grief said, 'When our son was alive, we often used to joke and say that we three could live on a desert island and be quite happy.' It seems to those who are left quite daunting to have to part with the dead. They get angry with anyone who merely mentions that they have to get through a final farewell, just as Peter was angry with us in the example in Chapter Two. They are bound up with the dead person in such a way that it seems almost life-threatening to them to have to let go of them.

In the grief, the ties to the dead are maintained. The thoughts, feelings and memories take up so much room that they become a replacement for the dead, although a poor and unsatisfactory one.

People in chronic grief usually have no resistance to tears, but the resistance does arise if an attempt is made to lead them into the profound weeping that is 'letting-go' weeping. They keep their breathing so rapid and shallow that the weeping remains 'calling' weeping.

Once the grief has become chronic, these people are hard to help. They desire grief therapy, are glad of the chance to talk about their grief and to weep in the group context along with the others, who they feel understand them. But chronic mourners are opposed to all actions which remove them from their grief. When in grief therapy we explain about the healing effect of weeping, they understand this to be an encouragement to continue their grief. In the worst case, the treatment can end up by further locking them into their role as mourners.

We have fairly good experience of helping clients who show early signs that the grief may turn chronic. These are people who are referred to us within the first couple of years after the loss and in whom we can see that isolation, anger with their network and bitterness against fate are in the offing, but not yet an established pattern. We have rarely been able to help clients referred to us several years after the loss. Possibly a longer-term therapy focusing on the clinging transference and the childhood experiences that underlie the symbiotic relationship with the deceased would make a final farewell possible.

Some therapists are worried about doing more harm than good when they are faced with a chronic griever. Our attitude is that a course of grief therapy is always worth a try in the case of non-psychotics. Grief therapy cannot be harmful (not, at least, for anyone but the therapists, who risk getting tired and frustrated; see also page 27).

The following is an example of a grief therapy which did not lead to the desired result.

Grief therapy for four-year-old grief after death of adult daughter

Yvonne (50) was referred four years after the death of her 21-year-old daughter Karen. The daughter had been a wheel-chair case for many years and lived with her mother. Yvonne was divorced and had no other children.

Yvonne had always lived a fairly isolated life, but after Karen's death she had also grown angry and bitter against her few friends and acquaintances, whom she felt did not understand her grief. When her friend forgot the anniversary of Karen's death, Yvonne was so hurt that she no longer wished to see this friend. Yvonne continued to cry a lot over Karen, but did not feel any relief from it.

Treatment

Our aims with the treatment were to break Yvonne's isolation (the third task) and start on the farewell to Karen (the fourth task). At our urging she wrote letters to her daughter about all she had meant to her and what her life was like without her. We got her to picture the kind of life her daughter would want her to have.

The therapeutic interventions had no significant effect. In the letters to Karen she related more or less the same story as she had told the group. She discovered nothing new. She knew well that Karen would want a happier life for her, but she could take no account of that. We suggested that she might feel that she was letting Karen down if she had a good life, but she repudiated that too.

We tried to get her to break her monotonous life, go to the cinema one day or have coffee with a friend, but nothing came of it. She was glad to join the group, where she felt that the other members understood her and where she could cry. But she never had a breakthrough in weeping, in spite of our usual briefing that she was to breathe out, breathe slowly and so on. Her comments to the others showed that her empathic ability was very slight. She spoke practically solely about herself.

Yvonne came to the group twelve times over eight weeks. Each time we pressed her gently to do something new in her life, and we used our imagination all the time to find new proposals for tasks. She rejected them all. Finally she concluded that we too had not understood the extent of her loss either and she left the group in anger.

Methods adopted

It is hardly necessary to repeat the methods here. The treatment must be regarded as unsuccessful. The client did not enter more deeply into the second task, did not get started on the third, and would not entertain the fourth task. As we gradually got to know her, it became clear how symbiotically over many years she had lived with her daughter, whom she had always overprotected. She had not processed the many losses which her life with a handicapped daughter had brought her, and therefore she could not cope at all with the great loss of her being dead. (This kind of problem is amplified in Chapter Seven, 'Losses of other kinds'.)

Yvonne did not have many resources. She had no training and only a slight network. If she had been going to process her grief over Karen, this would have meant 'a trip through the emotional desert', such as Pamela describes in her letter on page 127. Our attitude is that people on some level or other do what is healthiest for them in view of their personal resources and the support they have. Yvonne presumably had an intuitive feeling that she would not be able to manage the journey through the desert or to cope with all the everyday demands that would come when she no longer had the role of grieving mother. We think it was right to offer Yvonne the chance of grief therapy, as in a preliminary interview it is not possible to assess a client's resources. We have not been able to pick out any obvious defects in our treatment which might explain the outcome. So we have to conclude that we were too ambitious in assessing how far Yvonne was capable of getting. Her anger when she left the group was directed only at us therapists, so we must hope that she took away with her from the grief group a good experience of being in the enriching company of some other mourners.

Chapter six

A course of grief therapy – a personal account

In the following, Janet describes a course of grief therapy which she underwent after the suicide of her husband Adam. She sought out the therapist (referred to here as T) six months after her husband's death. She was concerned about her children Kirsten and Mary. At their father's death they were 9 and 7.

The grief therapy extended over seven months with weekly sessions. We have chosen not to comment on the account but to leave it to the reader to assess when and how Janet was working on the separate tasks of her grief work and how T's interventions acted.

On the telephone I told T what was the matter. One of my daughters, Kirsten, had begun to behave babyishly, but only when I was around. I thought I felt reasonably all right myself, so I was puzzled that the children were now beginning to get worse. But perhaps it was related to my husband, who died six months ago. 'I haven't much knowledge of children', said T, 'but I do know about grief. I have a vacant appointment for Friday at 10.15.' I tried one last time. 'Shall I bring Kirsten with me?' 'No', said T, 'I think we ought to talk first.' I told Kirsten that first of all the psychologist only wanted to talk to me. She immediately got very upset. I scarcely had it in me to console her, but I pulled myself together. Kirsten just cried and clung to me. How I wished there could have been someone else able to take over my job as mother. It was so incredibly stressful and unpleasant just to hold her. I wondered if I really was fond of her. But now at least I had to pretend I was fond of her.

At the first interview I explained to T that Kirsten had problems with learning her tables, couldn't do arithmetic, just the few sums she had to do seemed quite beyond her. Writing compositions was a nightmare. It had gradually come about that I was obliged to sit beside her and dictate. Kirsten cried and thought all my suggestions were daft and she wouldn't... and couldn't. She had also begun to talk baby talk. She often cried for a long time – whole half hours. It was not an upset kind of crying, but a pay-attention-to-me kind. T broke in: 'Can you easily hear the difference?' 'Yes, I have no difficulty in doing that.' The problem is that I can't bear to spend time comforting her. I get incredibly restless, confused and can hardly stay still to comfort her. But if I try gently to ease her away, I get a terribly bad conscience, and it isn't long anyway before Kirsten finds something else to cry about. And so we're back to square one.

But something that puzzled me was that there were very often episodes when I quite spontaneously criticized Kirsten for something that was quite unreasonable even from my point of view. But although I decided that I'd be better just not to say anything, it was only a matter of time before it happened again. It might be whether her hair should be plaited or be left loose. Quite surprisingly, T said, 'You can't cope with that until you have learned to pay heed to the child within yourself.'

I did not understand a word of this, but I suppose it takes time to get familiar with psychologists' language. I was going to tell about Mary, but T went on, 'Tell me, why do you focus solely on the children?' That was a surprising question. Hadn't she understood at all what the problem was? I just replied, 'I don't know.' I felt reasonably all right. Of course it was odd that I wasn't really upset that Adam was dead. But it was worst at first, when I was embarrassed about not being upset. And I wasn't happy about anything either. But then there was certainly nothing to be happy about. Listening to music, singing myself, enjoying the sunshine, having a good time with the children, all things I had enjoyed before, had now become things that hurt and which I avoided.

Suddenly, right out of the blue, T asked, 'What would you say to being given some homework for next time?' I nodded and said I was willing. T explained that I was to go home and write a letter to Adam in which I was to tell him everything I had not managed to say. 'Does that sound right to you?' I was surprised, both at having to write a letter to Adam, who was of course dead, but particularly at the last question. It seemed to be meant sincerely, not an order camouflaged as a polite question. If the work wasn't right for me, we would be able to change the content. That was a nice sensation.

When I had got the children to bed, I sat down to write. Without my noticing, the time was after midnight. I had only written Dear Adam. It was strange. What had I been thinking about for those three hours? The next evenings passed in the same slow way.

The next time T asked with interest how I had got on with writing. I had to admit that it had been difficult, but I had such great problems with concentrating. Every time I began to think about exactly what to write, my thoughts began to scatter. When I finally managed to get the pencil on to the paper, then the episode I was going to describe suddenly seemed quite trivial. Much too trivial – perhaps too embarrassing – to write down. It seemed as if it was easier and less committing just to think the thoughts.

One thought that constantly made itself felt was that Adam ought to have waited to take his life until Kirsten had come back from the school camp. It was unreasonable that she had left without Adam saying a proper goodbye to her. He didn't even go to see her off at the main station – just stayed at home. But there wasn't anything in it. Why was it so important anyway? One day more or less. Whether he managed to say goodbye or not. He hadn't said goodbye to Mary – or me – either.

Somehow I would liked to have written about everything that, in the days before Adam's death, I had done and said directly to annoy him. But I sort of didn't dare. It might be used against me. It would have been an enormous relief if I had been able to say it to Adam. But to write the fatal sentence that was the cause of Adam's suicide was quite simply impossible. Then I would have given myself away. If only I had never said it. I was just furious and disappointed when he said that he had decided to go to work to get some letters finished off. For we had just made up our minds to help each other and to give work in the home top priority so we could get it over and done with.

Adam's excuse was that he hoped to feel better when the most important things at his work were finished. I knew from experience that it wouldn't turn out like that. So it burst out of me: 'Just you try coming home this evening and telling me that you don't feel up to doing anything!' Adam didn't feel up to it, and never came home. I didn't get so much written, but did do some thinking. That was both pleasant and unpleasant.

The sentence was always in the foreground. I must have gone into a reverie, for from far away T was asking quietly and cautiously, 'Where have you gone to?' I tried to explain, but it was new for me to talk about things that so lacked concreteness. I said that I felt I was on a steep mountainside, and I had just got a footing with one leg, but the other leg and the rest of my body were on the way down into a deep black hole in a well that was quite narrow. From the side of the well there were partitions into the hollow chamber. The sides of the well took up more and more room in the chamber, so I had to take up less and less. When I woke up in the mornings, I lay completely rolled up and ached all over from lying curled up. It was impossible to lie stretched out. It simply hurt. It felt a bit different during the day. If I just moved quietly about and spoke softly, I managed. Then there was just about room for me. But if I just started to sing, smile, run down the stairs, call to the children, then it would immediately hurt. In such situations I came to take up more room and touch the partitions. T took a good time, looked thoughtful and nodded. It seemed she understood what I meant.

Before next time I was to write about what happened in the days around Adam's death. It proved to be a terrible experience. It was far worse writing about it than I remembered it being when it had really happened. The hopeless and all-alone-in-the-world feeling was now quite unbearable. I could well remember that for a brief moment I had had the same sensation when, at eleven in the morning, two and a half hours after Adam had gone to work, I contacted the police. How was I going to persuade anyone that the emergency services should go into action just because Adam had not phoned home. We hadn't even had an arrangement that he would. And even though I had left a telephone message for him to ring home, that was not alarming.

That morning, when I had asked Adam how he felt, I knew he was lying when he said 'fine'. Normally Adam would always make things a bit worse than I thought was necessary. At the same time I noticed that his hands in a way did not belong to him. He did not have contact with them. The police asked me to be calm and wait and see till closing-time. I was always welcome to phone or go there. They tried to calm me by saying that they had often known of people turning up. While I was writing I noticed a feeling of being incredibly small in a huge universe. I was puzzled that it was so much worse writing about the event than I remembered it being in reality.

The police phoned about 11 p.m. They had found Adam's car. The keys were in it, and one window was open. The police could not search with dogs until it was light again. That was odd to think of. Just because the sun set. It might mean that Adam would die before they found him. Another thought suddenly struck me. Imagine if Adam had suffered brain damage, would I be able to cope with that? I was quite sure he had taken an overdose of sleeping-pills.

'Had Adam taken an overdose?' asked T. I didn't know. I hadn't asked. It didn't matter. Adam was dead, anyway. 'Can't you get it sorted out before next time?' That was the worst thing I had been asked to do so far. Now I had to involve other people, and such a long time afterwards. It was embarrassing that I hadn't asked about it before. It might seem I didn't care that Adam was dead. I had read the death certificate many times, but it did not say anything. But now I would be forced to phone the police chief or county medical officer and talk about Adam's death. But one thing was sure, if T got the least suspicion that on the last day he lived Adam had written two cheques, she would at once set me to find out who had received them. And I just couldn't. To talk to the person who was the last to see Adam alive would be unbearable. I should be terribly jealous. I had a clear feeling that T was able to guess what I was thinking, so I hurriedly promised to find out how Adam had died, hoping that she would be content with that.

I chose to phone up the county medical officer, but was referred to the police chief. It was easier than I had feared. He was kind and understanding and thought it a good idea to get things sorted out, as he put it. He did the talking. That was fortunate. For a huge lump was in my throat all the time and stopped me asking.

The next time with T something surprising happened. When I was going to tell how Adam had died, I couldn't. I talked around it a bit. How they had found him. How high and how dense the trees were. I imagined that T could guess the rest. I pulled myself together and jumped into the deep water. I don't think I managed to say more than Adam died by.... before I was crying. T took my glasses off, gave me the box with tissues. If the worst had to happen, then it was nice that T apparently took it calmly. Perhaps she had been expecting me to cry. That was how it seemed. When I was beginning to get lucid again T asked, 'Why did you get upset?' Once more I pulled myself together violently: 'Because I am upset that I won't see Adam any more.' 'No, he is dead, and you will never be seeing Adam any more.' When I heard the word never, I started crying again. I felt it was the worst word she could use. Why had T suddenly turned so spiteful? Had I annoyed her without knowing anything about it? Nobody else would dream of saying things like that. It all passed off so quickly and was so different and unreal that it was impossible for me to manage to collect myself before she sat down on the sofa beside me, put her hand on my shoulder, and went on with her calm, monotonous stream of unpleasant words. 'Adam is dead, it is a pity for you, you have lost him for ever; you will never see him, you are in a bad way.' I felt most like shouting straight into her face, 'Shut your trap!' But I didn't. I couldn't stop crying. All was confusion. 'Just go on crying. You need it,' she went on. 'You have cried too little in your life.' How did she know that? She was right enough that I hadn't cried much, but then I hadn't had much reason to. I was one of the lucky ones. I had had a lucky and easy life without sorrows. And besides, it was no help despairing once the misfortune had come – on the contrary. I was confused. It seemed as if I had no control over anything. Was T angry with me? Half of the sentences she was saying were definitely very cruel. But her tone of voice pointed in the opposite direction. And I couldn't stop crying either. I thought of mental torture in the Soviet Union. T was certainly quite opposite to everyone else I knew. The more I cried, the more satisfied she became.

I must remember to buy some tissues for T. I had used up a good many of hers. That was embarrassing.

'We shall have to have a contract,' said T. 'As long as we two are meeting, you must promise not to commit suicide. What you do after that is your own affair. Is that a contract?' I said yes, but that was evidently not enough. 'Look at me while you're saying yes.' Now she had got me. I knew that trick. My mother had also made use of it. I had felt it to be mean and very unfair.

T now asked whether there was someone I could tell how I had felt around Adam's death. I thought and tried to think concretely. It was hard. It had to be a person who could understand what I meant. It was also important that the person would not get upset. It was necessary too for it to be someone who liked Adam. Finally Andrew came into my mind. He had written a letter to me when he heard about Adam's death. It was a good letter. I knew that he would be able to understand me. Some years ago his son had been run over and killed, and I remember that I then talked a bit to him about what it was like. When I suggested Andrew, T said, 'You think it's a good idea? He will be able to understand you? You'll have chatted to him before next Friday.' This sentence was said in the imperative. I said 'yes', though I didn't feel much minded to do it.

I had gradually got a clear impression that T was not going to get directly involved with Kirsten and Mary. I had to see to that myself.

I had not connected my own condition with Adam's death. I believed that my not being able to concentrate on reading the newspaper, watching TV, going to the theatre, reading, listening to what other people said were all connected in some way with poisoning, perhaps the wrong diet, maybe contact with chemicals, sprays and so on. It is true that I had always been very careful about avoiding those things, but I might be especially allergic. I had pondered going to a health farm where the food was specially cleansing to the body. But I did not really believe in it. It would not be very long before my workplace would find out that I could not grasp or take the initiative for anything. But some time would pass, perhaps a whole year, as I was quite good at pretending. If anyone spoke to me, I could not look at them, that was too much. I grew nervous that the other person would find out that I could not follow the conversation. It was better when I was the one talking. But there were gradually more and more things I couldn't do. I rarely managed to fill in a Giro paying-in slip correctly. They were always sent back; I had either forgotten the signature, the account number or perhaps the cheque endorsement – all things that other people just laughed at and called carelessness. But I wasn't careless – I just couldn't do it. If I made an appointment, I couldn't remember it until I had got it written down. I couldn't go shopping without a list – I just couldn't think what was needed, and it was next to impossible to make a shopping-list. When I had found out that we were out of butter, I had forgotten it was butter as soon as the refrigerator door had been shut.

I had come to terms with not sleeping very well at night. I woke up punctually at 3.50 every night and was wide awake. The worst of it was that when I woke up I had nervous stomach ache. After Adam's death I had been given a tranquillizer to go to sleep with.

The next Friday I told T about my meeting with Andrew. I had been on the verge of tears when I arrived and he put his arm round me. But I think I managed to pull myself together before he discovered that I was upset. 'Why wasn't he supposed to see that you were upset?' asked T. I didn't know. It would be very embarrassing for me, but it would also be a distressing situation for him to be put in. Anyway, I wasn't accustomed to crying. Apart from when I hurt myself as a child, I can remember only six times I cried when others had seen it. Three of them were connected with Adam's death. I was also embarrassed when other grown-ups cried. I had no idea what to do. I had told Andrew that I wasn't feeling too good just now. 'We were talking about how you might be coping, and we agreed that if anyone could cope then it would be you.' I was very sorry at not being able to live up to their expectations. I had disappointed them. T asked me what I told people who asked how I was. I might say, 'I'm not feeling so well, or I have felt better.' 'You must say I am unhappy, because that is what you are.' I thought it sounded affected. I tried to envisage how various acquaintances of mine would react when I said I was unhappy. And imagine if tears came to my eyes! All the girls could be ruled out at once. I imagined them touching me to comfort me. The mere thought turned me sick. With men – at least some of them – it would be different. Most would simply not be able to cope with the situation, and I would be disappointed and have a lower opinion of them. But what about John? I often chatted to him; he was not 'afraid' of my utterances; he believed what I said, even when it was unpleasant; he took me seriously and understood what I was saying. He was one of the few people who did not change his voice and speak in a hushed tone when he was talking to me in the period after Adam's death. He phoned a couple of days after Adam's death and said, 'What a mess! But you can ring me any time and ask me to do anything at all.' It felt incredibly kind and I felt he really meant it.

No, John did not try to deny the facts, even if they were unpleasant – quite the reverse. So when before long T asked whom I would dare to tell that I was upset that Adam was dead and perhaps even show I was upset, then I had John. I fixed a time with John for Wednesday evening. I decided that I would also show the article about grief. I gave him a copy so he was a bit prepared. So if the worst happened to me, then he could at least read that it was a normal reaction.

Tuesday night I was ill: diarrhoea, vomiting and stomach ache. When the children had gone to school, I went to bed. I drew the curtains and pulled the quilt over my head. The sun was shining right on to my bed. It was very unpleasant. It hurt. No doubt that was how Adam had felt in his bad periods. And I had not understood a thing! I had stubbornly tried to get him up and out into the sunshine to begin to do something. How unkind I had been. But that was how I had always thought it should be. If anyone felt a bit poorly in the morning, then make haste and get up, even though it was bad getting started. That helped. All my life my mother had lived that way. Had woken early in the morning and hurried to get up, make coffee and smoke a cheroot, and then be active from early morning.

Actually, there had recently been several episodes when I came to feel that I was suddenly understanding a good deal about Adam. On the one hand, it was a calming feeling to be able to sense how Adam had felt in many situations. But on the other hand, it was a terrible sensation to think that I had lived with Adam for twelve years without understanding how he really felt. Why had I never wanted to listen to how Adam felt? Why did I always have to explain it away and hurry to find something activating to do. And that was how I was with the children too. If I had the least impression that they were upset, I persuaded them that it was not so bad as they thought, and quickly thought up something nicer they could be doing and thinking about. To see them upset has always pained me so much that it would only be a few seconds before I intervened. But now I knew better. I was feeling in my own body how unpleasant it was when someone tried to get me away from gloomy thoughts by telling me that really I was quite all right. Finances in order, sensible and well-behaved children, good work.... so the problems I had weren't really there, or at least were insignificant.

I had to phone to put John off. I told him that I didn't feel well, was upset, had stayed home from work and was in bed. It didn't seem to affect John. He just stated that he would come as arranged and 'you know me well enough to know that I can stand seeing you upset'. It sounded nice when he said it, but there was something wrong all the same. Was I afraid of John not being able to stand it if I should cry? I couldn't really imagine being properly upset, not even alone. So perhaps it was something in myself, too.

It is different with T. It doesn't seem to bother her in the least that I cry and feel like hell. Not that I mean she doesn't care or is pleased. But as if it doesn't hurt her.

I told T a couple of weeks ago how Kirsten had adopted a new behaviour pattern. She might without warning suddenly start crying violently over something quite trivial. She might, for instance, ask how to spell some word, and if I didn't answer at once, did not hear what she asked, or perhaps spelt it differently from how she had, she suddenly turned quite unhappy or maybe furious. She cried, ran up to her bedroom, slammed the door and cried so loudly that she was sure I could hear it. Of course I went up to comfort her. When I tried to touch her and

143

console her, she kicked and punched and shouted that I was to go away. Then when, very reluctantly, I went, she again began to cry as if I was to come back again. One day when both she and I were calm and reasonable, I asked her what she wanted me to do when she was in that mood. Kirsten didn't know. She explained that when she was crying and I wasn't there, she wanted me to come. But when I came, she wanted most to go on crying, and she couldn't when I was there. When I told T about the episode, she reflected a bit, and said, 'Kirsten is a healthy child.' It sounded favourable, but I realized that T did not mean the same as I did by the word 'healthy'. She suggested that I should sit down beside Kirsten when she cried, but not say anything, not console her, but just be there. In a way I realized that this was the right method. I knew it was me who had to have the worst, perhaps almost impossible, job of seeing Kirsten crying and feeling rotten without being allowed to do anything. When it happened again, and Kirsten rushed up to her room in tears, I gathered myself together, considered and gave myself good time. Before I went up there, I took a strong drink. I had a feeling that that would make it easier. I sat down on the bed and did nothing. Kirsten cried. It was an eternity before I thought the weeping was becoming a bit more 'friendly' and approachable. I tried to put a hand on her shoulder. It was too soon. Her tears started up again. I thought, that's how you feel when your heart is bleeding. The time felt endless, but suddenly Kirsten began to come closer, and now she was receptive. In no time she was sitting by me and I was able to put my arms round her. It wasn't long before she began to talk and was in good spirits, as if nothing had happened. I was puzzled by the sudden change. She skipped down the stairs and her voice was happy. But why was it so horrible for me? Would I be able to get used to it? T seemed to have been born with it. I had a feeling that I could learn it. I decided: next time I would not have a drink first.

It quite often happened that the phone rang and I thought it was Adam – just for a moment. And a couple of times I had heard the phone and was sure it was Adam, but there was nobody on the line. But I did not take episodes like that to be anything special, just imagination or just old habits. For it was only for fractions of a second that the unpleasant feeling lasted, or perhaps the pleasant feeling. I was often pleased when I caught sight of Adam's car or a similar one. One day I had even waved to someone I thought was Adam. But then I did feel embarrassed. But there was no doubt that T had a definite idea of what the right way was. Grief was the right way, whereas emptiness, which in T's opinion had something to do with imagination, was wrong. To my mind, it ought to be the other way round. Grief is to me the worst thing I can imagine. Even the word is unpleasant. Deep down inside it seemed as if I knew that T was right. I recalled a remark from my childhood. I was at my aunt's funeral. When it was over, and everyone was saying goodbye, my grandfather said to some people who were saying that it was a shame for uncle, 'Now Freddy [my uncle] must just have peace to grieve for forty days.' I was at the time particularly puzzled that the words were so cruel, but that my grandfather's tone was so good and loving. At the same time he said it as if it were an obvious remark, an eternal truth. It did not fit together. But although I did not understand it, I realized that my grandfather was right. He was a wise man.

As I've said, T had several times tried to persuade me that I should show to others that I was upset that Adam was dead. I had got the impression that it might even be necessary for me to cry when other people could see it. And it was also important for Kirsten and Mary to know and see that I was upset. It sounded so obviously right and straightforward when I was with T, but the reality was different. I could certainly understand that Kirsten and Mary might get the idea that I was not at all upset that Adam was dead, and that was not true in spite of everything. But when I got home I could not carry it out. If I was buttering bread and thinking of Adam, I might well start crying, but the instant I heard a child on the stairs, I was outwardly myself again.

Perhaps it was the most difficult thing I had faced. I had to show and say to other people that I was upset. And it was right, when I was with T and sometimes when I was alone. But when there were others present, my upsetness vanished like lightning. I had returned to my old condition where both I myself and others knew me. Could I possibly learn it? To hold on to the upsetness would require that I should at least be able to keep away all other influences, including most of my own thoughts. And of course that was pretty impossible as long as I could not concentrate. And it was just as obvious that the only place it was possible was with T. There there were no other influences than hers and my own. And as soon as T noticed the least sign that I was upset, she was there at once, blowing life into the little spark, and before I knew it I had been weeping for a long time.

I had been thinking that at some point I might sell Adam's Volvo. It was fifteen years old. We had last driven in it in the autumn half-term. I began to spend some time thinking of the pros and cons of having it, but it seemed as if I did not want to get rid of it. Without realizing it, I happened to tell T that I hoped to find a letter from Adam in the car. I had also imagined that he might have sent it by post, and that it had gone to the wrong address. It might take a bit of time before it got re-addressed to me. But after eleven months that possibility was hardly reasonable. But there was a chance that the letter was lying in the car. It was strange, for I had never looked in the car. But in any case I would not find the letter if I got rid of the car. T asked without further ado, 'What does the letter say?' I had not a moment's doubt: 'Dear Janet. I am sorry it has to end like this, but I think it's the best way out – for you too. I know you will be able to cope. Love Adam.' 'Lean back and breathe right down in your stomach.' This was a trick T had. It worked every time, and I began to cry. I pulled myself together to stop crying, but T was there at once. 'That's good, just go on. You need to cry.'

'Well, now we've finished for today, and you'll have got rid of the car by next time.' There was no reason to reply. It was not a question. The answer was obvious. I got up, rather bemused.

But it is not so bad in T's presence. She has a quality which is hard to describe. It seems as if she is neutral towards my bad – perhaps also towards my good – qualities. She does not ascribe any value to them – is not judgmental. It seems as if she merely registers soberly the facts of the matter. This quality means that I find it easy to relate what I am feeling and thinking. There is no reason to find out first what I want T to think about me in the particular situation and then afterwards say what fits. I am becoming more honest than I have ever been. Not in the sense that I used to lie – constantly. But rather that I skated around my bad qualities. Sometimes with the result that the quality or episode filled my head completely. Latterly I had begun to wonder a bit whether it might be the reason for my lack of concentration. Maybe all my energy was going into concealing that it was my fault that Adam had taken his own life. I wondered if T's tolerance would stretch that far. For she knew nothing about it being my fault. Would she suggest I went to the police? I had a clear impression that she wouldn't. But what? If I had been a believing Catholic, I could ask for forgiveness, confess. Would that help? Within the last few weeks I had had a dream, or rather three dreams almost alike. I was driving in my white van and Adam was lying in the back, very ill, perhaps dead already. A man I didn't know ran into the back. I got out of the car and he came up and told me off for killing Adam. Adam got up and told him, 'It's not Janet, but I myself.' Yes, that was typical of Adam. He could never think of putting the blame on me, although it was obviously my fault.

For the first time since Adam's death Kirsten and Mary were going to be at home alone. They used to be able to be on their own while Adam and I went, for instance, to the theatre, cinema or a concert. But it had been quite impossible after his death. It seemed to me that they were afraid I was going to die. And I was too. So it was so hard, perhaps impossible, to resolve it. For it might happen. We had drawn up a piece of paper on which we and Marjorie were to decide where they were going to live, and so on, if I died before they were 18. But their insecurity had far from vanished. So, against that background it was lovely that they were both asleep when I got home. But Kirsten woke up and came down and slept with me.

A couple of days later, Mary and I witnessed a drowning accident at the lake. When we got home, Mary sat down to play with an electronic game. I saw at once that she was fighting her tears. If only T had been here. She would certainly have been able to deal with the situation so that something good came out of it. I had a clear feeling that the situation was important. I went over to Mary, made her stand up so I could sit down. She did not protest, as she would normally have done when I disturbed her game. This confirmed my assumption that she was just pretending to play. For a long time I said nothing. I collected myself, mustered courage, 'Mary, do you feel like playing?' I asked. She shook her head, and was close to tears. 'Are you thinking about Adam?' Mary nodded. I told her how Adam had left home that Wednesday morning, and gone to a wood where nobody could find him until it was too late. I talked for a long time with Mary about what she could remember from that day.

I had fetched her from the recreation centre. I had thought that I would immediately have told her that Adam was dead. But instead I asked her how she had got on at Hannah's. Mary told me that she had dreamt that I was dead and had woken up because her pillow was wet and there was nobody to comfort her. I was struck dumb. I said no more. When I got home, I said she was to come into the living room. I was going to tell her something very sad. The words came out, 'Is Adam dead?' She remembered nothing of all this. But she did remember that she thought it was strange she didn't cry. Suddenly Mary said: 'I've got a headache.' 'It's sad for us that Adam is dead, don't you think?' Mary battled with her tears. But she did not succeed. I said, as I imagined T would have said, 'Just cry.' But I couldn't say it as T would have said it. Mary let the tears flow, but there was no sound. I could feel Mary becoming rigid. She answered, 'I can't cry. It was like when Grandad died.' I asked whether, when she was awake, she still thought that Adam was here. She nodded, and said that it was like when her class teacher at school was ill; then too she dreamed that the teacher was well and in school. I said that I often missed Adam and asked if she did too. She nodded.

After Adam had died, I sometimes asked the children if they missed Adam or thought about him. They always shook their heads. So this had to be regarded as progress. Mary lay down and fell asleep.

At my next appointment with T I told her what a terrible time I had had getting rid of Adam's car. T said, more or less casually, 'You certainly make a thorough job of things.' There was no deciding whether this was good or bad. It was just a statement of fact. But though a lot was like hell, there was something that had improved. Once in the last week I had had a very positive experience with Kirsten. Several times during the day she usually has to sit with me. It ends up with me either getting irritated and asking her to go, or just easing her gently away, and then

Kirsten just walks restlessly around and can't settle to anything. That gives me a bad conscience and I easily get cross with her. But this time something nice happened. I put my arms round Kirsten, just as usual, but suddenly it was warm and nice. It was quite plain that the warmth was flowing. Kirsten must also have noticed the difference, for she got up of her own accord. First she went and played the piano. She suddenly felt like it, she said. Then she went humming out into the kitchen. She then did some arithmetic in columns, which usually gave her trouble.

Last time I was with T she asked whether Adam had a grave. He had, but I had not had a stone put up. The children and I had looked at gravestones, but we had not been able to agree. T had thought that I should find one during the next fortnight. It was odd, because this time the children and I quickly agreed. I had decided to go to the stonemason myself and tell him what the inscription was to be. I had a feeling that my voice would tremble and I would get tears in my eyes. But there was no getting out of it.

Gradually I had often taken to going to bed when the children had left for school. That was the best thing, in spite of everything. Draw the curtains, unplug the telephone and get right down under the quilt. On Wednesday, 4th May, when I was in bed, I dreamt that I was with my mother in my home town and Adam had promised that he would not die before a certain date. The 5th May and Adam's name were written in gold on a red ribbon, which was set with blue and white flowers. My mother and Adam were out in the kitchen. I was nervous, but was looking forward a bit to talking to Adam. The gist of it was that if I spent sufficient time on Adam, he would give up dying. I was quite sure I would succeed.

A fortnight had passed since I had been to T. It must have been a tough fortnight. I cried almost without a break at T's. On the way home I gave up the idea of calling in at the stonemason. It was too daunting.

About a month ago T had asked if I had any pictures of Adam on display. The only one was a silhouette which hung behind the door of my bedroom. 'Why not in the living room?' 'Nobody must know that I like Adam,' I answered. T then suggested that I should put a good likeness of him somewhere where I could often see it. T asked me to bring the picture with me next Friday. I wondered if T was curious and wanted to see what Adam looked like. I looked out some pictures. It is always a bit hard to imagine what someone you don't know looks like, so I chose various pictures of Adam so that T could better imagine what he was like.

I now had to look at one of the pictures and tell what Adam had been like when I took the picture. I don't remember anything except that I wept constantly. But it dawned upon me that I had had the picture standing beside my bed for over a month without looking at it. It was a tough hour. I went straight home and to bed. I woke with Mary trying to awaken me. It was very long since I had slept so deeply. I felt relaxed in a nice way. Tony came visiting, and it was quite nice. I was actually glad he came. The next few days several little things happened which were good.

I also 'felt like' going to Adam's grave and planting flowers. Would everything be better from now on? When I called on Jane, she saw at once that I had begun to feel better. It is nice when someone else notices that my condition has genuinely improved. Then there is firmer ground under your feet. Perhaps I am getting through the grief. I wonder if that means that I shall now be able to think of Adam without it being so terribly unpleasant. I wonder how I find out if the grief is over. And how shall I feel? Will I have to be upset for, for example, four hours and then forget it and feel good for the next four? It has also dawned upon me that the reason I couldn't (wouldn't) talk to other people about Adam is that I have just begun to notice that I was both fond of him and hated him. That's why I think it must get easier to talk about him. I just have to say what I feel, and that is at least easier than saying what I ought to feel, or perhaps rather what I think other people think I ought to feel.

After a fortnight I was feeling pretty low when I went to T. I told her all my tale of woe. My shortcomings as a mother, that I could never manage to go to work, that the house is quite impossible and much too big. My finances quite confused. And my mother who phones and urges. I could see that T was concentrating. Suddenly she asked in a brisk tone: 'Are you ready to do a job of work?' It sounded as if it was to wash the floor or clean the windows. Of course I said 'yes'. She went into the next room and emerged with a towel, which she knotted. I was to kneel down on the floor, take the towel, and raise it over my head and thump it down as hard as I could into some cushions. I did it a couple of times. Then suddenly T began shouting in an unpleasantly loud and shrill voice. I was to say, as I thumped the towel down, something about Adam having to leave me and not cling on to me. And I was to say it in the imperative.

I began to cry. T shouted, 'Stop crying!' It was odd, she was normally pleased when I cried. Of course my weeping was mostly a grizzling, pay-attention-to-me crying. But all the same. It was quite clear that T was showing a different and cruel side. At one point I was quite exhausted by thumping and collapsed in tears. T asked me how I felt. I probed a bit. Much had changed. I was relaxed, tired, and the 'ball' that had been in my stomach had gone. I suddenly felt a very great gratitude to T. I believe I only took hold of her knees, perhaps her hands too, but when I did it, I was pervaded by a feeling that I would give T everything I possessed.

I walked on air down the stairs and home. The birch tree had come out. I had not noticed that before. It was so fantastically lovely. I lay down and looked up at the leaves. Fancy anything being so beautiful. Much had suddenly changed. While I lay looking up at the birch, I knew that I could throw Adam's old raincoat away. I also realized why I had not wanted to go along and help the police to find Adam. I would not accept that Adam was dead. I also knew the reason why I hadn't sent in the bill for the funeral to be settled out of the estate. I would be able to do it now. We had supper out on the terrace, not because the weather was good but because I felt like it. That was something quite new. I felt like doing things. A delightful sensation. Nor was I nervous at the thought of someone turning up. The thought of having sole responsibility for the children did not take my breath away.

But by Monday I realized that this was not going to last. I could feel that I was on the way down again. It begins with my becoming confused at having to get through so much, but not being able to cope with it. Everything becomes insurmountable. My bad conscience at not understanding Adam is being replaced by the fear of feeling the same way. I have an immense desire to be irresponsible, for someone to look after children, work, house, finances, solicitors. But the children are by far the most important. I feel I am no good at all as a mother. I shall have to give up my work. The house takes all my strength away. Even when I have unplugged the phone I can hear the phone ringing. After a couple of days I have stopped sleeping and yet am not tired. I stop eating. It is all like the state I was in when Adam died. Next time I told T about my condition and the resemblance to my state a year before. I also told her that, if it had been today, I would have gone myself to identify Adam and not let everyone else make me so afraid and confused.

T asked me to sit comfortably and relaxed in the chair and close my eyes. I was to imagine I was at hospital outside the room where Adam was lying dead. I was now quietly and calmly to enter the room. I could feel the tears running down my cheeks. I began to tremble. T said that I could take her with me if I liked. I took a good time. When I finally got to the door, I lost my courage and went back again to fetch T. It was much easier the second time with T. I opened the door and left T standing outside the door, while I entered the room and closed the door. For I could always go out and fetch her. I looked around the room, as T had asked me. It was all white, or rather light-coloured. There were no windows or lamps, but the sun was shining in there. Adam lay in the middle of the room in a white bed. I could only see his face, arms and hands. Adam had no wrinkles on his forehead and looked relaxed. I thought that of course the wrinkles were my fault and so they had now disappeared. Adam was wearing a ring, which sparkled green. I was surprised, as Adam never wore rings. But it was very beautiful. When I felt I had seen what I wanted, I went out and sat down on the chair. The tears had been trickling down all the time, but the trembling had passed off when I had taken T with me.

T now suggested that the next night I should imagine that I had been given a bed at the hospital in a room beside where Adam was lying dead. I was allowed to go in there as often as I 'felt like it', all night until 8 o'clock the next morning. I was to tell Adam everything I had regretted and repented of and had a bad conscience about. I was to phone T the next day and tell her what had happened. T asked if there was someone I could ask to sleep with me at night. I thought about it. I did not feel like it. I had enough to do looking after myself.

I don't know how many times I went in to Adam that night. But after a couple of times when I was upset, wept much, I embraced him and told him some of all the unkind things I had done to him. Not in order to be unkind to him directly, but rather out of fantastic thoughtlessness. But after a few times I began to get a bit aggressive and had a feeling that it was not just my fault. As the night wore on, it became quite clear that Adam had contributed to the way things turned out. In the morning when I phoned T it felt very embarrassing to say I had become aggressive. But T took it calmly and commended me for a good piece of work.

In the afternoon I felt like going for a cycle ride round the lake. I had often thought that it was odd that since Adam's death I had never been round it. Before, Adam and I had walked there for hours in the hope that Adam would feel a bit better. But now suddenly the desire was there. I even thought that it was lovely there. I was able to enjoy the birds and the trees. Odd. And delightful.

(After Janet had written this account for the book, it turned out that she had not yet written the farewell letter to Adam. It turned into several farewell letters.)

23 August 1986

Dear Adam,
It is not easy for me to get beyond 'Dear Adam' – tears and thoughts.

Four years and two months have now passed. It feels like a very long time. A whole life. Everything has become quite different – in one way – but in another it is the same. It is hard to explain. But the world looks different. I see in a different way. Much more. A broader angle. I take in films, theatre, ballet, books, music, people, in a larger way.

I have always looked upon friends as white and enemies as black. I can now feel that it has been strenuous. To accept that I too have some 'dark' areas is an incredible relief. Not to need to hide it. But there's no doubt a long way to go yet. I still have a great propensity for awarding whiteness to my friends and blackness to my enemies. The picture I had of myself as the one who was always happy, had time to spend with everyone who expressed a wish for it, could cope with almost everything and took responsibility for everything and everyone has crumbled away. It was tough and anxiety-filled. Feeling I was worth nothing was terrible. But it was worth the trouble. How our relationship would have been and developed with my present insight is impossible to say, but it would have been different. I now see plainly that in that area we suited each other like hand and glove. I became worth more the more responsibility I was given, and you felt best without responsibility.

That I have slowly learnt to notice what I feel like doing is quite fantastic. I have simply never thought that I might feel like doing something independently of those around me. It was against nature. If you felt like going to the cinema with me, then I felt like it too. I don't remember ever being able to give my opinion first. And not until now have I seen through the 'badness' of this. I often let it be seen that I was doing it for your sake. When I still sometimes put my foot in it with Kirsten and Mary, they're on their guard at once. I can plainly feel that they don't want to be burdened with my bad conscience. The fact that I can feel what I want and don't want and act accordingly has had a great effect upon myself. I feel that when I now am what I am, and someone still likes me, then it is me they like and not, as before, what I did. That has meant that I have come to have a far better relationship to some people. But, on the other hand, I have to regret that it has also meant that many people have gone away from me.

As I gradually show more and more sides of myself, the same thing apparently happens with those around me. It is an incredibly fascinating phenomenon. As I still find it far easier to notice how other people feel, it is often the case that, by 'mirroring' myself in others, I discover how I am and feel myself.

Responsibility and guilt have been interwoven. I took responsibility, and if things went wrong it was my fault. It almost looks as if I couldn't do without that guilt. The guilt has gradually retreated into the background in step with my handing over the responsibility which does not belong to me. In connection with your suicide, for several years it seemed plainly my fault. Now the guilt has disappeared. It was you who made the decision and so it was your responsibility. But I was jointly responsible, because together we 'rowed in deep water' during the fifteen years we lived together . . .

Now, when one of the children is feeling bad, I can use my
energy to do something useful for them instead of feeling like hell.
It has had the effect that both can be upset, furious, and other
unpleasant things without my feeling bad.

I think – particularly at times – that the price for what has been
achieved has been high. Losing you. Was it really necessary?
When I think over it, how lovely it would have been if you had
lived and felt as I do now. Was it really necessary for you to die, if
I was going to be able to wake up? The more I think, the clearer it
becomes. Yes, it was. So much was needed and nothing less could
do it. The crisis I ended up in gave me the opportunity to obtain the
insight I have today. With all the benefits – and drawbacks – it
brought with it.

The greatest price I have paid is the realization that my mother
has never liked me. This has caused and still causes great grief.
When at first I was 'working' on my mother, I believed that
everything would become happy if only this was put right. But if
things aren't happy, then it can of course not become so. Although
it is still linked with great sorrow, it is at least true . . . .

When I think back on the first forty years of my life, how often
have I cried? Fewer than fifteen times. And ten of them were in
connection with the hopeless feeling when you got depressed and
'disappeared' into another world. But now – just when I think of
you being dead, and I'll never see you again, the tears begin to
flow . . . .

I often think that Kirsten, Mary and you might have much
enjoyed playing together. I feel quite clearly that part of you can
never be replaced by anyone. There will always be a gap. That we
have Kirsten and Mary, and that we have them jointly and only us
and them – and you are not here . . .it is and will always feel so
unjust, unfair and cruel.

It happens more frequently that I can get angry with you for not
being here. When the thunderstorm broke over the river on our
canoe trip, I was angry you weren't there to tell us what to do. It is
quite unfair that I now have sole responsibility for Kirsten and
Mary. You just went away from it – just like that, and left it all to
me. I also get angry when I see how Kirsten and Mary have to seek
and get rebuffed when they try to have contact with an adult male,
which you have the main responsibility for fulfilling in them.

I am not much inclined to say goodbye to you as the wise one
who can bone up on everything. Often when I hear men holding
forth, I think: if only you had been here and could cut through the
nonsense and set everything to rights. I often carry on
conversations with you in situations when I myself cannot get

everything in order. And I have a clear feeling that you would be able to do it if you were present.

But another thing that appeared was love. I will not say goodbye to that in connection with you. Just to write it brings me to tears. It is quite unclear. But one thing is clear, I have never felt – or maybe rather I have never dared to feel – that anyone liked me fully and completely. I suppose it is a bit much to claim that nobody has been fond of me. But, as it were, only parts of me – the parts of me I have shown off. Maybe, to you I have shown the largest part of myself, larger than to anyone else. I don't know. But I miss terribly being loved and embraced by you. The picture that comes up is: a child (little) just being cuddled, warmly and lovingly, without being asked for anything in return.

Goodbye.

7 April 1987

Dear Adam,
Something suggests that I did not manage to say a proper farewell to our love. It is easy to deceive others, but impossible to deceive oneself – in the long run. The first time I got a feeling that something was wrong was when, about six months ago, I felt a great love for the first time after your death. The feelings took me by surprise – I was not prepared to 'defend' myself against them. I sort of let things take their course and watched the emotions. I saw a picture of a green meadow where the sun was shining unusually beautifully. There was a ground-mist preventing me from getting across – to love. Something connected with fear prevented it. The mist is still there. But I am getting some inkling of what the mist symbolizes, the one that prevents me from walking freely in the meadow and just enjoying myself. Among other things, it has something to do with you. I don't feel I can permit myself to feel love for another man, a love which is, besides, of quite a different quality from what I have ever felt. The love is free of the sensation of owning the other person. I can still be myself without being swallowed up – and without swallowing up. The baseless jealousy from which I have often suffered is not there either. When people criticize him, I can listen without taking sides. In some cases I agree, in others I agree less. But I apparently do not need to defend the love by denying his 'bad' sides.

I am infinitely grateful that by your death you gave me this possibility. But it seems as if I must not accept the gift. To have such great love for someone else but you. I know that you would accept – even with joy – my newly acquired feeling of love. In my imagination I often picture how delightful it might have been with

154

you. My love for you has been bound up with security and dependence. I think it is unjust and hard to face the fact that the love I so much wanted to have together with you, and which you have given me the chance of getting by sacrificing your life, cannot be used on us, and never will be. It feels cruel and unjust. Never more to be able to snuggle up to you and be held. Never more to feel security through your nearness, so nervousness and sorrows fade. To say goodbye to the love between us for ever. Suddenly I have an overwhelming desire to put a new stone on your grave. A stone which just says:

Goodbye dear Adam.

Chapter seven

Losses of other kinds

Any change in life contains potential for both growth and loss. But it is common for this relationship not to be recognized, and so there are many happenings which are not discovered as either growth or loss, writes John Schneider in *Stress, Loss and Grief*. A lack of recognition of loss is a source of stress. If the loss is accepted, the feelings of grief become accessible and the state of stress can be resolved in a healthy way.

If we realize that there is a connection between change and loss, then we also understand why so many people are puzzled at feeling disappointed and empty at times when they think they ought to be experiencing joy and satisfaction. Getting married, having children, being promoted, finishing a difficult project, are examples of changes which often entail invisible losses: the loss of freedom, the farewell to old roles, dreams, involvement and excitement, just to mention a few. What is known as a 'let-down' can follow hard on the intense joy and relief at having achieved our goal. The let-down is intensified and prolonged by our shame and guilt at not just being happy and relieved. Merely using the words 'loss' and 'grief' at all in this context is a provocation to most people.

'Success depressions' are relieved, however, by making room for recognition of the loss and thus room for a kind of grief work on the level that is necessary. That this is easier said than done is an almost essential rider to be added in a success-oriented society with an ideal of happiness in which even the more visible losses are not noticed.

We mention these fairly marginal losses in order to steer the reader into regarding losses as part of daily life. In this way we hope to open the way for an understanding of the many other ambiguous losses which both we and our clients are exposed to throughout life.

In the years during which our attention has been particularly focused on loss, grief and growth, we have become fairly convinced that many people are being let down, because their losses and traumas are being overlooked. Many therapists focus upon the more visible problems and thus give only superficial help. If the client were to be helped through the tasks of grief work, a more fundamental change would take place.

We will give a number of examples of areas where it may be beneficial to focus on grief work in connection with the ambiguous losses which entail many changes. The purpose is again to be able to identify and relieve pathological grief development.

Developmental crisis and grief work

In developmental crises, or what are called 'critical phases of life', there is also grief work. Puberty, the menopause, old age are examples of three phases where it is plain that a person has to bid farewell to one kind of life and greet the arrival of another. For most people this process is accomplished quietly and invisibly, but we do know that some have problems because they do not go through the grief work. In other words, they are troubled by a form of pathological grief. It would be possible to help these people by focusing on the four tasks of grief work and so identifying where they have come to a halt.

Around the menopause some women develop a state resembling chronic grief, because about that time they also lose their maternal function. Such a woman might, in connection with the first task, be asked to articulate the losses which her altered life has brought about. This might give an opening into the feelings of grief, the second task. The third and fourth tasks would then be more accessible, so that she would be able to welcome the opportunities she has now that she no longer has young children.

Depressions in the first years of retirement are common. One of the causes is presumably stress caused by unprocessed grief. If we consider how many losses a person sustains when he bids farewell to his workplace, there are strong emotions that are not released if he 'copes with' this change without taking the loss seriously.

The price is high. That is why there are probably many senior citizens who ought to be helped to focus on their grief work. The senior citizen might begin by sorting out what he is saying goodbye to in his working life, so as later to be able to give retirement a proper welcome. Senior citizen groups with this special focus are, to our mind, an obvious possibility.

In Norway the Norwegian-British sociologist Ken Heap is interested in the elderly and their losses caused by old age. He works with them both in groups and in individual therapy. Ken Heap considers it probable that a number of dementia states in old people may be seen as unresolved grief at dead spouses, dead friends, lost opportunities and so on. They become depressed, withdraw from the world and live behind their senility, which is often kept going by tranquillizers and anti-depressants. Ken Heap's experience is that, if they are given help to focus on the feelings of grief, old people too can gain life-giving strength.

From our open grief groups we have no experience with losses linked to critical phases of life. But it has been thought-provoking to experience how clients with other ambiguous losses, like divorce, handicap and possibly terminal illness, have been helped on their way in their grief work by bereaved people who had to put a 'tombstone' over someone who had died. Clients with ambiguous losses thus were given support to erect a tombstone too.

Grief work with ambiguous losses

We shall give here three examples of grief therapy, with a blind man, the mother of a handicapped child and a woman with muscular atrophy. When working with the handicapped, it is an advantage to keep the four tasks in mind in order to assess whether the client has come to a halt in his grief at the handicap. A pathological development of grief may be because the handicapped person has not recognized that it is a loss at all. The first task has not been done. It may be that he recognizes the loss at a certain level but is so afraid of feeling 'weak' that the pain and anger are shunned. The second task thus becomes a problem preventing the handicapped person from grasping the energy to be found in the fourth task.

All therapists in the area of handicaps know the costs involved when energy is bound up in the handicap. Some people develop symptoms like depression, emptiness and an aggressive attitude to others. They feel isolated and try desperately to compensate for their handicap. Other handicapped people are threatened by a chronic state of grief and so primarily get stuck on the third task, that of acquiring new skills. The consequence is often that they grow bitter and self-protective, and develop an invalid's attitude to life, which may not be entirely necessary.

Grief therapy and a chronic handicap

Thirty-six-year-old Jeff had been blind since he was 6. He was referred to us because his marriage to a sighted woman was breaking up. Jeff had become more and more difficult to live with. There were two young children of the marriage. An interview with his wife made it apparent that the conflict was largely bound up with the fact that Jeff's state had deteriorated since they had had children. He was offered a course of treatment, and this developed into grief therapy focusing on his handicap.

Jeff had grown up in a family where he had been well helped with his blindness on the outward, practical level of schooling, training and so on. But the family had never talked about his handicap, because it was important for them 'not to feel sorry for Jeff'. He himself had done all he could to live up to this attitude. In every way he had tried to compensate for his handicap by throwing himself into all kinds of activities to prove to the world and those close to him that he was 'normal' in spite of his handicap. His dread of feeling weakness had marked his whole life.

As time passed Jeff had developed a perfectionism and an aggressive attitude that were creating difficulties between him and others. In particular, it was spoiling his marriage.

It seemed possible to regard Jeff's symptoms as an avoided-grief reaction. In his fear of ending up weak and dependent upon others, he had repressed all feelings in connection with being blind. The third task would be for him to arrive at a relationship to his blindness in which he could talk about it and make reasonable demands on himself and those around him. The fourth task would give him strength to invest his feelings in other people in a different way from previously.

Jeff was presented with the suggestion that he should work on his losses from being blind. At first he was irritated and almost angry at being confronted with a demand to talk only about his handicap at the beginning. But the therapist stuck to it. She openly explained to him her assessment of his case, and instructed him as to what grief work is and the development it can lead to. Jeff appeared sceptical. He was given the assignment to go home and reflect whether it did not seem probable that this focus might be useful after all.

Jeff returned and had then accepted the contract. In the first session he told his story, which was of the blind child, the young blind man, and of his adult life with hopes, dreams and disappointments – a moving account, in which the therapist did not intervene but requested him to tell it to his wife at home. He told it without very many emotions, but it was new for him merely to articulate many of the old episodes from his life. He had got started on the first task.

In the next therapy sessions he related more and more episodes from his life as a blind man. At one time the therapist asked him what was the worst thing about being blind just then. He reflected for a long time, struggling to keep his emotions under control. Then, with the tears running down his cheeks, he said that the worst thing was that he would never be able to see his children. The therapist stuck to the subject and supported him by saying how hurtful this must be. For the first time ever, Jeff gave way to his grief. He wept long and deeply over his handicap and the deprivations he had suffered all his life.

The third task then interwove with the emotional process, for Jeff soon discovered that he was ready to open up and tell both his wife and family about his grief. In the first period after the breakthrough in the grief therapy he was, of course, worried at the thought that people at his workplace, would take note of his 'weakness'. At the therapist's suggestion, he managed therefore to tell the person closest to him at the office that he had started therapy. He had a lucky break straight away, as his colleague told him what a relief it was for her to be able to talk about Jeff's handicap. She told him that they had been worried because he never asked for help. That made them feel uncertain towards him. She also told him that they admired the fighting spirit that he possessed to overcome the problems involved in his handicap. That was the start of Jeff being able, in a small way, to ask for help with various minor tasks. By overstepping boundaries in this way he had started on the third task of his grief work.

The fourth task in such cases follows quickly by itself, for emotional energy is released by Jeff managing to say goodbye to a life in which he had constantly, on one level, tried to function like a sighted person. After that, his relations with his wife improved.

In essentials Jeff had now finished his grief work at having gone blind as a child and over the losses which his blindness had hitherto caused him. But that does not mean that Jeff had finished all his grief work. He lives with what may be called ' ongoing grief'. His handicap will continue to bring him new losses. In a few years he may discover that he does not get promoted, even though he is qualified. Later he may feel like changing his job and discover that there is no chance of this, or that, at best, the openings are very limited. When children-in-law and grandchildren come on the scene, he will not be able to see them either. So it is crucial for him to be sufficiently flexible to go in and out of his grief. He can then achieve the good quality of life which one sees in many handicapped people who have a natural emotional relation to their loss.

Crisis intervention: a mother and a handicapped child

Gillian bore a child with Down's syndrome. In the first months of the child's life she recognized intellectually that the child was handicapped, but denied it on the emotional level, and this was a problem. She maintained that it was her child and that she loved it even though it had Down's syndrome. At the time of the birth she rejected aggressively all attempts by the hospital to intervene.

Three or four months after the birth she became increasingly depressed and began to develop an unnatural dependence upon the baby.

Gillian had largely come to a standstill on the second task, and had need of help to make contact with the pain of having given birth to a mentally deficient child. Like many other parents of handicapped children, she was threatened by pathological grief. The parents' grief work is often complicated by guilt and shame towards the child, so they deny that there is any question of a loss. The Swedish psychologist Gerti Fyhr therefore calls the grief over having a handicapped child the 'forbidden grief'. Gillian's case had to be regarded as a delayed grief reaction in which she needed help to face up to her loss so that she could be brought out of her depressive state. She had lost the normal child to which she had been looking forward. She had had a mentally deficient child instead. If this grief work is not lived through, the relationship between mother and child is unnecessarily complicated. So Gillian was asked to write about the child she had dreamed of, and despite much resistance, that became for her the start of feeling her grief.

The goal of the four tasks is to be able to 'greet' (that is to receive) one's handicapped child in a way that makes it possible to develop realistic hopes about the child. Like Jeff, she has to live with an ongoing grief as long as the child lives.

Gillian needed help with the 'primary grief work' involved in recognizing that she did not have a healthy child. Gerti Fyhr calls this the loss of the dream child. By working through the primary loss, the way is opened up for going in and out of the grief feelings in the ongoing grief in a natural and so more life-giving way. The first grief work in connection with a handicapped child is, in other words, the turning-point that means that one can live with the ongoing grief.

Parents of handicapped children have to go through grief work of various magnitudes at various points in the child's life. They lose one hope the day they are told that the child cannot go to a normal school. Placing it in an institution is not only a farewell to everyday life with the child, but for a number of parents it symbolizes the loss of having a handicapped child. So we see dramatic crisis situations when they are placed in institutions.

If someone can go in and out of the emotions of grief, he is able to bid farewell to a hope that was shattered and later acquire a new, realistic hope. Parents with chronic or avoided grief do not have the same flexibility. They therefore find it hard to reach a relationship with the child in which there is room for hope and joy as well as disappointment and grief.

With these two examples from the area of handicap we want to inspire therapists to become more aware about identifying a pathological grief development. So we repeat that if, in handicapped people or the parents of handicapped children, we encounter symptoms like depression, fear, a tendency to isolation and bitterness or over-compensation in relation to the loss/trauma, it is worth investigating whether the person has worked through his grief.

Losses and traumas, and life-threatening illness

People who have their first thrombosis or for whom cancer is diagnosed are confronted with their own death. But for most people the notion is so filled with fear that it is evaded as quickly as possible. Therefore there are a very large number of people who never manage to articulate their thoughts and feelings. Particularly in the Western world there is a kind of collective denial, which means that people only talk freely about death on a general level. Patients with thromboses and cancers 'don't die'; the topic has become taboo, because it has become much too concrete.

That it why there are many of these patients who develop all the symptoms we mentioned when describing pathological grief development: fear, depression, nightmares, isolation, bitterness or a hectic activity resembling the over-compensation of handicapped people. This denial of the loss/trauma in connection with life-threatening diseases is stress-inducing. John Schneider, who is particularly interested in the connection between stress and illness, writes: 'Unresolved loss may be one of the most significant factors in physical health and disease. It can be a source of stress that overburdens people to the point that they are paralyzed. If the stress reaches over-whelming levels, it often prevents them from carrying out even routine tasks.' Conversely, grief work means that the stress is reduced and thus physical and psychical force is regained for fighting the consequences of the illness.

The four tasks of grief work in relation to life-threatening illness

The four tasks of grief work with illnesses that may well prove life-threatening can be set out in the following way:

First task: The recognition that the illness can have consequences such as handicap or death.

Second task: The pain and anger that this should come upon *me* in particular. The emotions at the curtailment of life which the illness threatens. Grief at perhaps having to leave one's children before time. These are examples of emotions that may be usual in this task.

Third task: The acquisition of the skills required if one is going to be able both physically and mentally to live with having 'one's illness with one'. The ability to make use of a network is important.

Fourth task: The energy is shifted from anxiety about the future to life here and now.

This is naturally a long process requiring both personal resources and support from others. The goal is for someone to be able, at intervals, to live as Elizabeth Kübler-Ross expresses it: 'If you begin to be able to see death as an invisible but kind companion on your journey through life, reminding you not to wait until tomorrow to do what is important for you today, you can learn to live your life instead of passing through it.'

In the grief group we have had a number of people both with handicaps and with serious illnesses like sclerosis and cancer.

A woman, Sonia, aged 25, was referred to the group in connection with the crisis that was triggered off when she was diagnosed as having muscular atrophy. In the grief group she worked on facing up to her illness and the frightening prospects ahead. At first Sonia was quite rigid in her fear of the future and had great difficulty in being alone with her thoughts. The recognition of the consequences of the illness soon unlocked emotions, so that over a couple of months she managed to weep and rage about her illness. The most hurtful thing for her was that her child would have to grow up with a handicapped mother, a mother facing an early death.

The third task in Sonia's case was intensive work to distance herself from her father, who had always indirectly dominated her by requiring her to protect him in every way. Thus he let her know that he was suffering more from her illness than she was herself. Her old feeling that other people's feelings were more important than her own became a crucial theme for her in the group. So she was given the assignment of writing a letter to her father in which she described all her feelings in relation to her illness and told him how hard it had been for her to tell him of her diagnosis. The letter was not to be sent, but opened the way for her to start altering her relationship with her father and subsequently with other people too.

Sonia's history is an example of the therapeutic process we describe in Chapter One. Through grief at one's illness, and grief at all the sacrifices she had made for her father over the years, she found strength to look after herself and to fight against her illness in a different way from before.

The fourth task was primarily to strengthen her ability to get as much as possible out of life here and now. She decided to give notice at work, which she had never enjoyed. By means of sick benefit and an application for a pension, she arranged her affairs so that she was able to be with her child more and got time to take up various interests which she had never had time or means to make a priority before. Happily, her husband accepted the plan and backed her up.

Participation in the group also came to mean that she began to be able to use her friends in a better way than before, when she had always been the helper. This was crucial for her 'welcome' to a life as a handicapped person.

Hope, grief work and life-threatening illness

Hope is an essential part of everyone's life, both healthy and sick. Hope is such a natural part of our existence that we do not notice how many times during just one day we feel and express hope. We hope it will be sunny tomorrow so that we can have a good time on the beach. We hope that our spouse will come home in a good mood so that we can spend a cosy evening together. We hope that a difficult matter at work will be successful. We hope that our daughter will pass her exam. We hope that our baby will be born perfect. We hope that our influenza will soon pass off. If we grieve, we hope at the same time that the pain will gradually get less. If we did not have the hope that the pain would fade with time, very few of us would be able to endure the feelings of grief. Hope is the driving force when we choose to go on fighting.

The importance of hope becomes even clearer when we look at people with a chronic or life-threatening illness. People talk of seriously ill or very old people 'giving up' and lying down to die. In other words, they cease to hope. They stop believing that tomorrow may bring new good experiences, however small these may be. When dealing with possibly terminal illness, we may find it a serious problem that so many people equate grieving with giving up hope.

Very few people are not made afraid by the prospect of a slow death in which they will have to battle with handicap and pain. If the diagnosis is cancer, people feel disquieted. Statistics show that some cancer patients die within five years, others survive.

A woman who had had one breast removed because of a tumour, told us:

> I was living with unconscious fear. When the sun shone and I was in secure and good company, it vanished. When the clouds were black and I felt alone and insecure, the dread crept into me. It came from unknown places and crept up on me without my realizing at first that the dread was 'in the scar' from my breast operation. On check-up visits to the hospital I could understand better where the anxiety came from, but it did not go away, even though the doctors

told me that everything was looking normal. I began to feel quite 'neurotic' – I walked around and was afraid for no reason – the doctors were telling me that I had been healed.

About a year passed. One day I met a young doctor at a chance check-up. He looked as if he could stand hearing about my 'crazy' fear. The doctor asked me what I was afraid of and reassured me by saying that if he got cancer, he would sometimes be afraid as well. Suddenly it all poured out of me. I told him in tears that I feared an evil-smelling sick-bed, which I knew that some cancer patients had when the metastases could not be stopped. I feared death and was terrified at the thought of having to say goodbye to my family.

The doctor listened and I cried and cried. When I at last looked up, I could see that he had tears in his eyes. He said again that he understood me, and that it was good for me to cry, and that I should go home and tell my husband in detail what I was afraid of. If my husband did not dare to listen to me, I was to force him to and demand that he should listen to me. Otherwise he could tell me that all my tests looked fine, so my prognosis was good.

Since then I have talked about my fear to many different people. I have even described my own funeral to a woman friend who could stand me crying. My anxiety has gone away, and I don't feel 'neurotic' any more. If my cancer does break out again, I hope that I can overcome it. That is my basic feeling toward the disease which, in some way, I still have with me.

Many doctors do not realize how healing to the soul is the process described by this woman who had had breast surgery. Thanks to the young doctor, her husband and friends, she became able to live with the illness 'like an invisible companion through life', to use Kübler-Ross's expression. Doctors are often so set in the notion that 'you mustn't deprive the patient of hope' that they overlook the patients' fear of the future.

The story of the woman who had had breast surgery shows very clearly that a doctor who dares to unlock the fear *does not deprive his patients of hope*. On the contrary. The dread of illness and the fear of death are altered and, at best, vanish when we are given a chance to share our thoughts and feelings with others. For most of us, they cannot be borne alone. The young doctor gave the woman invaluable help by being able to absorb her emotions and not being scared by the thought of a 'nervous breakdown'. Unfortunately, 'breakdown' is often confused with weeping copiously. At some hospitals the tranquillizers are brought out as soon as the patients begin to cry.

It is depressing to think that by remarks like 'There, there, you mustn't look on the gloomy side; it will all work out all right!' we may cut short the very conversation which the sick person needs to be able to let go of his fear. If people who work with or live with patients would only understand this connection, a great deal of genuine joy would find its place alongside the pain and restrictions which any terminal illness brings.

In our grief at what we risk losing lies the germ of joy at what we have. Through grief at what we have lost develops hope for what we may have in future.

When the fatal illness is in active development, we begin to enter ongoing grief. But even in this phase there is hope. If someone is allowed to weep at having had a difficult night in hospital, there will be room for hoping that the next night will be easier. If we permit ourselves to feel grief that our muscular atrophy is now so bad that we have had to take to a wheelchair, then there is a better chance of hoping that this stage will be as full of contentment and will last as long as possible. If we permit ourselves to grieve because it looks as if we shall die in hospital and not at home as we had expected, then there is room for hoping that our son in America will come over in time to see us before we die.

It sounds so platitudinous to say 'Where there's life, there's hope', but it is a profound truth. Hoping is so vital a part of being human that wherever there is a spark of life left, there is also a hope for something, whether it is merely to be able to sit up in bed today or to smile at one's family. Grief over what one has lost and life-giving hope go hand in hand.

Contact with dying people can teach us that there may be a lot of life in short-term hopes. It is therefore true that we must never deprive people of hope.

That the dying person at some point must have peace to die, to abandon hope, to wind up his contacts and thus say goodbye is a problem area which we have chosen to leave out in this book. The process of dying is not part of ordinary life-giving grief work.

Losses, traumas and AIDS

Of recent years the disease of AIDS has been frightening both therapists and the general public. The number of cases is rising; as yet there are no possibilities for treating actual AIDS-sufferers, and there are many misunderstandings about the way AIDS is passed on.

Both AIDS-infected healthy people (often called HIV-positive) and actual AIDS sufferers need help to talk about their thoughts and feelings. But the fear of infection means that they are often abandoned by both therapists and their network.

So let us stress that AIDS is only passed on by sexual contact and by getting blood from an AIDS-infected person into one's own blood (usually by using the same injection needle). There is no risk of infection in normal human mixing. AIDS is not infectious through saliva or tears, and so you can with an easy mind put your arm around an AIDS sufferer who is crying. Even if both the AIDS sufferer and the therapist have a wound, and these wounds should come in contact, there is no risk of infection. There has to be a greater quantity of blood for someone to be infected.

We shall not go into details about actual AIDS patients, as help for them is no different from help to others with terminal illnesses. They have to learn to 'live with death and die with life'.

The group diagnosed as HIV-positive is in a special situation. It is not known how great their risk is of developing actual AIDS. As we have said, they are carriers of the infection and must therefore change their sexual habits. They discover that many people from their network withdraw from them out of fear of being infected. They have to go through grief work to be able to return to a life with a changed outlook for the future.

On 24 and 25 January 1987 the newspaper *Information* published an interview with 25-year-old Bo, which well describes the four tasks of grief. Bo tells how on the day he received the diagnosis HIV-positive, a glass wall came down between him and those around him. For eight months he went about alone with his thoughts about AIDS in a sense of unreality. His first actual reaction was the feeling of loss: 'A sense that I never again could do this or that,' he recounts.

> I couldn't understand that I was the person involved. I didn't feel ill, and yet the test showed that I was antibody-positive.
>
> At first I believed that I would be able to get by all right. I had had the strength to stand up and tell my parents and friends that I was gay, so I would be able to cope with this. But, hell, I couldn't! Finally I put an advert in the magazine *Pan*, which is published by the Association of Gays and Lesbians. I wanted to contact others who are HIV-positive.
>
> It was something of a relief to have a chat with others who were in the same situation. I joined in a weekend seminar where all the participants were HIV-positive. Funnily enough it gave me a boost to face up to the problems. To me at least it was overwhelming to see the guts people have even though they have been branded: possible AIDS-sufferer.

The relief at sharing his problems with others who were in the same difficult situation gave him energy for a different attitude to life.

> I take one day at a time [he says, and continues] I have become

much more attentive to the signals from my body – whether I am getting stressed, getting too little sleep, etc. The days are over when I can just keep driving on at full speed.

My life goes on as before. But with a greater awareness that I shall have to die one day. Everyone has to die – that little mechanism is built in to life. But it suddenly comes very close to you the day you're told that the test was positive.

One of the losses that an HIV-positive person has to go through is the sexual restrictions which follow from the danger of infection in intercourse. But if he gets through his grief work, we know that there are possibilities for development, even when the problem area is AIDS. Bo describes his new sex-life as follows:

I have had some very fine and intense sexual experiences since I have begun to take preventive measures seriously. And safe sex is everything you can ask for – as long as you just avoid getting semen into your body.

It may well be that it is necessary to cut down on the more rough-and-tumble sex, and for people to learn to touch each other more. I actually think that more variations have entered into my sexuality since I have had to use a condom. It's a matter of getting the imagination going.

Naturally it was not easy for Bo to clarify his mind like this. The emotions of grief require hard work to get through – work which we have now spent a whole book describing. But 'funnily enough', says Bo, 'it gives you a boost to face up to the problems,' and with that quotation we think it right to close the last chapter of this book.

Concluding reflections

Over the ten years we have been engaged in grief therapy, there has been a noticeable change in our therapeutic work as a whole. Our encounters with people who find it hard to cope with their natural healing grief work, together with Alice Miller's view of the unprocessed losses and traumas of childhood, have gradually given us a new basis for planning a course of treatment.

We have discovered that often when we are faced with people with general mental troubles it is an advantage to take our starting-point in their unprocessed bereavements and thus help them to make contact with their grief work. This relates to what Alice Miller calls 'the true self' in a way both natural and comprehensible to the client. We believe that focusing on grief as a universal human emotional process which heals psychological wounds mobilizes the client's resources in a vitalizing and fairly rapid way.

In the last chapter we mentioned a number of the ambiguous losses which one may look for in drawing up a plan of treatment. The critical phases of life contain obvious opportunities for getting the grief work started.

We would also like to remind you how an emotionally deprived childhood can be conceived as a loss – loss of love and understanding, as Alice Miller describes it in her books. Any grief work from adult life eases access to the grief at having to abandon hope of ever getting the unconditional love and acceptance that was missed out on in childhood.

So, as often as possible we begin a course of therapy with a piece of grief work and return to this theme many times during the treatment. Naturally, we use other therapeutic methods concurrently.

We have come to the conviction that precisely because grief is a natural process, a profound knowledge of healthy grief work would be a good basis for everyone who wishes to learn to work therapeutically. A deep understanding of what losses and traumas do to us human beings is not only a way for us to understand many of the symptoms which people seek help in overcoming, but also a creative focus for treatment. It teaches therapists to start out from the individual client's psychical resources and helps the client to a more realistic assessment of his true potential, because focus on grief work is a focus on health rather than illness.

At this point we would suggest that the reader re-reads Chapter One, 'On attachment, loss and grief', as the reader now has a much better background for understanding the theoretical concepts discussed there.

In 1985 we attended the first international conference on grief, held in Israel. One of the themes there was that the grieving person is a stepchild both in psychology and psychiatry. Presumably this is because both clinical psychology and psychiatry have concentrated on symptoms which expressed a deviation from the normal. Grief work is a normal reaction and so has not been subjected to deeper analysis, apart from early mother–child attachment and the consequences of separation. Naturally we hope that this book may contribute to giving the 'stepchild' a higher standing with psychologists, psychiatrists and other therapists in the social and health sectors.

Over the last fifteen years it is true that many therapists have been taught how to help people in grief and crisis. The result of this teaching has been that many are able to recognize grief and crisis states requiring support. However, it is our experience that there is a great feeling of impotence among GPs, staff in hospital wards and social administrators when they are faced with complicated bereavements. What help should be offered, and who has the available resources to help?

Being trained as a professional helper implies that one ought to be able to cope with crisis and grief help. However, helplessness is the feeling that is often evoked by a meeting with a grieving mother, a despairing widower or a person with a serious medical diagnosis. The grieving person feels that only a return to the situation before the loss will be able to console him. To a therapist, helplessness is probably one of the most provoking feelings. He is being paid to help, not to be impotent. Impotence therefore results in paralysing therapists so that they neglect the important work of assisting when strong emotions have to be expressed and when the private network has to be mobilized. Dare we? Can we? Will we? are the questions one could ask.

The answer is complicated as long as the social and health sectors do not do more to train their personnel in working with grief and crisis. So there is a need for opportunities for referral. The help must be free of charge, and there must not be waiting lists, because quick help is double help.

We consider that, with some authority, we can recommend the open grief group as a treatment option for individuals with severe, complicated bereavements which, if left without preventive intervention, might develop into mental or physical illness. We have tested out the method for ten years on about 950 clients. For the last five years we have been training therapists in leading grief groups themselves at their respective workplaces and have supervised their work. In this way we know that it is possible for therapists with some therapeutic experience to learn the method and that it can be used at many different kinds of institutions.

When training other people to lead grief groups, we have employed a model that includes three months of practical experience in a grief group led by us with subsequent supervision of their own grief-group work. Our trainees also feel that working with grief has had an enriching influence on their other therapeutic work.

Our vision

During their lives everybody undergoes serious losses and traumas. Some have sufficient emotional resources and a network adequate to cope with the grief process without professional help, and obviously such people must not be turned into patients. Normal grief should *not* be treated.

There should be an option available to the many individuals who find themselves in trouble because they cannot cope with their grief without help. This would obviate much human suffering and, owing to the preventive aspect, would be a good investment for society.

In England they have been working for many years with self-help groups for the bereaved. Those who have themselves undergone the loss of a child help others who are now in the same situation. For instance, widows and widowers help others who have recently lost their partners. The idea of bereavement service is widespread, in connection with both hospitals and churches. It is an offer to mourners of an extra network in the difficult period after the loss – a network with special qualifications for helping, because it consists of people who have been in a similar situation.

In Denmark too we have a number of self-help group organizations on the English pattern. However, they have proved not to function if one or more of the members remain stuck in an unresolved grief reaction (delayed, avoided or chronic grief).

Therefore, help for the bereaved cannot be merely put in the hands of private help organizations. In the case of people with complicated losses – for example, suicide – then in each large borough or at several places in each county there ought to be offers of open grief groups led by specially trained therapists. These can be set up either within the social security administration or within the district psychiatric service. The best thing would be if the groups were a collaboration between the social services and the district psychiatric service. It is therefore encouraging that in Denmark grief groups led by professionals trained in the open grief group method are being set up locally, primarily in conjunction with the social services offices.

One example of the use of the open grief group method under psychiatric auspices is the neurosis hospital of Montebello in Elsinore. Here, for a three-year period, they have been training doctors, psychologists and nurses in work on grief therapy and crisis intervention. Each ward now has an open grief group as a treatment option for those patients whose symptoms are assumed to derive from a pathological grief development and for those patients who are hospitalized in connection with a loss they are unable to process by themselves. These groups have proved to be a valuable treatment option, and the staff have been given some therapeutic tools that have had an effect on the whole therapeutic environment around them.

The family systems and rituals in our society are often inadequate to help people through the four tasks of grief work. Our vision is that it ought to be possible for any citizen who is affected by severe, complicated losses, and is left exposed and in despair with a shaky basis for their life, to be referred to a place where he can find organized grief help, if his network cannot provide the required support: a *life-raft*, as our clients at one period dubbed the grief group. At some point in our lives we may all find ourselves needing a life-raft.

With this we take our leave of our readers, who have naturally been in our thoughts as we wrote. We imagine that our reflections upon grief and the encounter with those people who in this book have shared their heart's-blood with the reader have given material for reflection about the basic emotional processes that affect us all.

So a meeting may have taken place and, as we hope it will leave traces, we want to close with Shakespeare's lovely words in *Julius Caesar* concerning the leave-taking that is not necessarily the final farewell:

For ever and for ever, farewell, Cassius!
If we do meet again, why we shall smile;
If not, why, then, this parting was well made.

References

Bowlby, J. (1969, 1973, 1980) *Attachment and Loss*, vols I–III, New York: Basic Books.

Cullberg, J. (1983) *Krise og udvikling*, Copenhagen: Hans Reitzel. (Not available in English.)

Davidsen-Nielsen, M. and Leick, N. (1990) 'Open grief groups: individual short term therapy focusing on complicated losses', *Group Work* 2: 187–201.

Deutsch, Helene (1937) 'Absence of grief', *Psychoanalytic Quarterly*.

Engel, G. (1961) 'Is grief a disease: a challenge for medical research', *Psychosomatic Medicine* 23: 18-27.

Erikson, Erik H. (1968) *Childhood and Society*, New York: W.W. Norton.

Freud, Sigmund (1940) *Trauer und Melancholi*, collected works, vol. 10, Imago.

Frey, W.H. (1980) 'Not-so-idle-tears', *Psychology Today* 13.

Fromm, Erich (1956) *The Art of Loving*, New York: Harper & Brothers.

Kübler-Ross, E. (1969) *On Death and Dying*, New York: Macmillan.

—— (1975) *Death: The Final Stage of Growth*, Englewood Cliffs, NJ: Prentice-Hall.

Lowen, A. (1983) *Narcissism: The Denial of the True Self*, New York: Macmillan.

Miller, Alice (1986) *Thou Shalt Not Be Aware: Society's Betrayal of the Child*, London: Pluto.

—— (1987) *The Drama of Being a Child and the Search for the True Self*, London: Virago.

Parkes, C.M. (1972) *Bereavement: Studies of Grief in Adult Life*, London: Tavistock.

—— (1985) 'Bereavement', *British Journal of Psychiatry* 146: 11–17.

Ramsay, R.W. (1979) 'Bereavement: a behavioural treatment of pathological grief', in P.O. Sjüden, S. Bates and W.S. Dockens (eds) *Trends in Behaviour Therapy*, New York: Academic Press, pp. 217-48.

Schneider, J. (1984) *Stress, Loss and Grief*, Baltimore, MD: University Park Press.

Simonton, O.C., Matthews-Simonton, S. and Creighton, J.L. (1978) *Getting Well Again*, Los Angeles: J.P. Tarcher.

Worden, J.W. (1982) *Grief Counselling and Grief Therapy*, London: Tavistock.

Yalom, I.D. (1980) *Existential Psychotherapy*, New York: Basic Books.

Index